SEXUAL VICTIMISATION

Sexual Victimisation

Two Recent Researches Into Sex Problems and
Their Social Effects

Edited by
D. J. WEST
*Professor (Emeritus) of Clinical Criminology,
Institute of Criminology,
University of Cambridge*

Gower

Published by
Gower Publishing Company Limited,
Gower House, Croft Road, Aldershot,
Hampshire GU11 3HR, England

and

Gower Publishing Company,
Old Post Road, Brookfield,
Vermont 05036, U.S.A.

Reprinted 1986

British Library Cataloguing in Publication Data

Sexual victimisation: two recent researches into sex problems
   and their social effects.
   1. Child molesting--Great Britain. 2. Girls--Great Britain.
   3. Homosexuality, Male--Social aspects--Great Britain.
   I. West, D.J.
   362.7'044   HQ72.G7

Library of Congress Cataloging in Publication Data

Main entry under title: Sexual victimisation

   Bibliography: p.
   1. Child molesting--Great Britain. 2. Sexually abused
children--Great Britain. 3. Girls--Great Britain--Crimes
against. 4. Homosexuals, Male--Great Britain. I. West, D.J.
(Donald James), 1924-   . [DNLM: 1. Child Abuse.
2. Homosexuality. 3. Paraphilias. 4. Sex Offenses. 5. Social
Problems. HQ 71 S5186[
HQ72.G7S48 1985   362.7'044   84-28981

ISBN 0-566-00832-7

Printed and bound in Great Britain by
Paradigm Print, Gateshead, Tyne and Wear.

Contents

List of tables

List of figures

Preface

D. J. WEST

This book sets out the results of two studies of two very different problems of sexual life. The first concerns behaviour that is forbidden by law, custom and the moral sense of the overwhelming majority of contemporary society, namely sexual contacts of adults with very young girls. By questioning grown-up women about their own recollections of such incidents when they were children, it was hoped to obtain some realistic indications of the prevalence of this form of deviant behaviour and of its repercussions upon the feelings of the girls involved, both at the time and in their later life. In the second study, a sample of men of self declared homosexual orientation were questioned about the problematic aspects of their life style, and in particular about their confrontations with police and other authorities. Their behaviour, although deviant from that of the heterosexual majority, is illegal only under particular circumstances, and does not attract moral condemnation so universally as does child molestation.

The two studies have come together fortuitously, because they were being carried out at roughly the same time at the Institute of Criminology. It cannot be argued that they appear on the surface to have much in common, save perhaps in encountering similar methodological problems of sampling and securing sufficient replies to an initial questionnaire. Nevertheless, the findings of these very different enquiries raise some of the same underlying issues. They each draw

attention to the fact that criminal statistics about sexual
misconduct reflect no more than a tiny and probably untypical
fraction of what is actually happening in the community. This
raises the question of the effectiveness of the criminal law
as a weapon of social control. The results of the homosexuality survey, in particular, show how informal methods independent of statute law exert a coercive pressure towards
conformity with established values. The desirability, effici-
ency and psychological cost of these informal controls, compared with formal legislation, are issues of some dispute, in
relation to child sexuality as much as in relation to homosexuality. The unpleasant things that reportedly happen to
some small girls when it is disclosed that they have been the
object of an adult's sexual attentions, or to some young men
when their homosexual inclinations are revealed to their parents, highlight the reasons young people have for keeping
their own counsel. The cruelty and insensitivity with which
problematic sexual matters are often handled calls into question the justification for the methods of enforcement commonly
applied, which appear as a damaging over-reaction. The findings of each of these studies have something to contribute to
the debate.

   Other issues brought out by both investigations include the
plurality of values in contemporary society and the varied
importance and meaning attributed to the involvement of young
girls in heterosexual acts or to the commission of homosexual
acts between males of any age. Religious teachings, feminist
concerns with sexual oppression, clinical and sociological
studies of the varieties of sexual behaviour and their consequences, to say nothing of the force of tradition, all have
different things to say, and all have some influence on public
opinion. Sex educators are hard put to it to provide an
agreed, coherent and rational scheme for the guidance of the
young.

   In reporting their findings the investigators have been cau-
tious in pursuing questions of policy far removed from the
factual material they collected. They deliberately concentrated on the analysis of the information obtained from their
subjects, and its immediate practical implications, without
pursuing wider and more controversial issues. To fill the gap
a concluding note making some suggestions about what lessons
might be learned has been added.

Authorship

At the time this research was being carried out the contrib-
utors were all attached to the Cambridge University Institute
of Criminology as follows:

Ms C.L. Nash   Research Associate.

Dr N.L. Thompson   Visiting Fellow from the Department
                      of Psychology, Macquarie University,
                      New South Wales.

Dr D.J. West   Director and Professor of Clinical
                      Criminology.

T.P. Woodhouse   Student placement from North London
                      Polytechnic.

Acknowledgements

The exploratory study of sexual victimisation histories of young women followed from a proposal put to the Department of Health and Social Security by D.J. West in June 1981. The Department provided a grant which enabled the Institute of Criminology to appoint Ms C.L. Nash as a full time Research Associate for a period of two years, to complete the planning and to carry out the project in consultation with Professor West. The Department is not responsible for the results or for any opinions expressed.

The study of socio-legal problems of homosexuals was carried out on the initiative of Dr N.L. Thompson, using Institute of Criminology resources. The findings are the sole responsibility of the three authors.

Part I
Sexual molestation of young girls: a retrospective survey

C. L. NASH AND D. J. WEST

1 Background to the enquiry

THE NATURE OF CHILD SEXUAL ABUSE

Researchers have defined child sexual abuse in several ways. The most simple is perhaps, 'the exploitation of a child for the sexual gratification of an adult' (Fraser 1981). Kempe and Kempe (1978) elaborate, referring to it as, '...the involvement of dependent, developmentally immature children and adolescents in sexual activities they do not truly comprehend, to which they are unable to give informed consent, or that violate the social taboos of family roles'.

Despite the increasing awareness of the problems of sexual abuse of children little is actually known about the numbers involved or whether such experiences have effects extending into adulthood. Research has tended to deal almost exclusively with reported cases in which the police and/or social services have been involved. Moreover, it has been argued that children may not become aware of being victims of a sexual offence unless they become involved in court proceedings (Reifen 1958, 1973).

Confusion surrounds the area of consent, for whilst a child can be held legally responsible for its actions at age ten, the law holds that a child cannot give valid consent to sexual intimacy until the age of 16. Most people would tend to turn a blind eye where the under age sexual behaviour consisted of consensual peer group activity, but when an adult is involved the issue of consent is always problematic. Even if the child apparently responds willingly to the sexual overtures he or she may be doing so through fear of or obedience to adult authority. Steele and Alexander (1981) say, 'The adult instigator takes advantage of the child's own normal sexual responsiveness, his/her wishes to please and obedience to authority'.

The ability of a child to participate in adult sexual activity is a matter of controversy. Ample historical documentation exists to show that children in ancient Greece and Rome were used by adults for sexual purposes (De Mause 1974). In the Middle Ages also, sexual play between adults and children was neither uncommon nor considered to be scandalous (Ariés 1962). The detailed diary kept by the personal physician of Louis XIII of France indicates that as a child he was subject to the sexual whims of his own relatives and servants (De Mause 1974). This is unlikely to have been an exceptional case.

The concept of childhood being a period of innocence and vulnerability, needing protection from adult sexuality, developed only in relatively recent times. There is some evidence to suggest that even today some societies indulge in more liberal adult/child sexual relationships. For example, according to Ford and Beach (1952) South American Siriono parents masturbate their children.

In their famous studies, Kinsey et al. (1953) reported orgasm in a four month old girl and in a five month old boy. The descriptions appear to resemble closely orgasm in adults, but not everyone is convinced that the experiences are comparable. Modarressi (1980) asserts that, 'childhood sexual behaviour, no matter how closely it imitates the adult sexual experience, does not lead to the orgasm which is the goal of sexual relationship in adulthood'.

A child's capacity for full orgasm is less relevant than its ability to derive pleasure from some forms of sexual behaviour. There is ample evidence that children may show overt interest in and experiment with sexual activity from an early age (Schofield 1965, Janus and Bess 1981). Some research has identified a category of 'participating victims' who appear to be willing partners in sexual activity with adults (Weiss et al. 1955, Virkunnen 1975). Bender and Blau (1937) reported that, 'The history of the relationship in our cases usually suggested at least some cooperation of the child in the activity, and in some cases the child assumed an active role in

2

initiating the relationship'.

What constitutes active participation, compliance and enjoy-
ment in a sexual incident between an adult and child remains
disputable. It can be argued that, for informed consent to be
possible, a child should have attained both sexual and emotional maturity. This study includes all forms of sexual contact between a child and an adult regardless of whether or not
the incident was regarded as unpleasant by the child. For
convenience we have used the term 'child sexual abuse' as
others have done, to embrace all such incidents, but without
meaning to imply that they are invariably harmful or never
solicited by the child.

THE INCIDENCE OF REPORTED CHILD SEXUAL ABUSE

In English law any sexual contact involving a person of either
sex under 16 constitutes the crime of indecent assault under
the Sexual Offences Act 1956. Consensual sexual intercourse
with a girl under 16 is a separate crime, and nonconsensual
vaginal penetration is rape. Indecencies with or towards
children under 14, even if the offender does not actually
touch the child, but perhaps has the child watch or touch him,
are offences under the Indecency with Children Act 1964.

The Home Office statistics of 'crimes known to the police'
report the total numbers of offences of rape, incest and indecent assault without specifying whether the victims are adults
or children. Unlawful sexual intercourse with a girl under 16
or under 13 are the only recorded sex crimes that necessarily
involve children. In England and Wales in 1982 there were 223
recorded cases of unlawful sexual intercourse with a girl
under 13. Ten years before, in 1972, the number was much the
same - 256. Reported cases of unlawful sexual intercourse
with girls under 16, however, have fallen gradually from 5,129
in 1972 to 2,791 in 1982 (Home Office 1983). This decrease
may reflect an increasing reluctance on the part of the police
to prosecute if the male in question is, in fact, the girl's
boyfriend, or near to her in age and the intercourse was with
her full consent.

Walmsley and White (1979) conducted a close analysis of all
indictable sexual offences leading to the conviction of the
offender in the year 1973. The age of victim/partners under
the age of consent in the main offence categories involving
females is shown in Table 1.1.

American researchers believe that only a tiny and probably

3

Table 1.1

Percentages in various age ranges among victim/partners of
persons convicted of sexual offences in 1973
(Adapted from Walmsley and White (1979) Table B2)

Age of victim/partner

Offence	0-4 %	5-9 %	10-12 %	13-15 %	(Sub-total) 0-15 %	16+ %	Total cases (=100%)
Indecent assault on a female	3.2	24.8	15.4	26.2	69.6	30.4	2,551
Unlawful sexual intercourse	–	2.7	13.8	83.5	100.0	–	709
Rape and attempted rape	–	4.7	2.8	24.3	31.7	68.3	321
Incest and attempted incest	–	7.8	19.4	45.7	72.8	27.2	129
Total cases	82	677	525	1,397	2,681	1,029	3,710

4

unrepresentative sample of child sex abuse offenders appears in police statistics or becomes known to social agencies (Landis 1956, Chaneles 1967, Finkelhor 1979, Corwen 1982). Even so, American national yearly incidence figures are estimated at 36,000 such cases [1]. Home Office Criminal Statistics must also greatly under represent the real extent of the problem.

The subject is sensitive and until recently has been little researched. In Britain, the reporting of child sexual abuse, as with all crime, is not mandatory. In order to determine how many cases have become known to certain professional bodies, Mrazek et al. (1981) set up a study in which 1,619 members of Area Review Committees [2] were asked to reveal how many cases of sexual abuse with a child aged 15 or less had become known to them during the year June 1977 to May 1978. The 42 per cent of members who replied reported dealing with a total of 1,072 cases during the period. A perpetrator was prosecuted in 43 per cent of cases.

RESEARCH INTO THE INCIDENCE OF CHILD SEXUAL ABUSE

Previous research on child sexual abuse has paid relatively little attention to the question of incidence, probably because of the many practical problems in the way of an investigation. Any attempt to discover current cases, or even to study retrospectively the prevalence of women with a history of childhood sexual molestation, is fraught with difficulties. Questions tend to be intrusive of privacy and therefore individuals are reluctant to reply, perhaps feeling shocked, insulted or angry. For practical and ethical reasons, children cannot be asked directly. Memory failure over time, subconscious or even deliberate blocking, and the rationalisation or the reinterpretation of emotive childhood events, render problematic the interpretation of information gathered retrospectively from adults. Despite this, some retrospective surveys have been carried out on a variety of selected groups.

Hamilton (1929) found that, of 100 married women volunteers in New York City, ten per cent reported some prepubertal sexual experience. These included one instance of rape, two of attempted intercourse and seven of 'sexplay'. Little can be deduced from this, since the sample was of the 'snowball' type (consisting of friends and undefined groups with a relatively high level of culture) and may not have been at all representative. Moreover, the age of the male perpetrator was not indicated.

The earliest systematic information on intimate sexual habits is probably that gathered by Kinsey et al. (1949 and
1953). Of the 4,441 American women interviewed, 24 per cent
reported preadolescent sexual contact with an adult male. A
subsample of 1,200 women were asked more extensive questions
about their early sexual history. Of these, 333 (28 per cent)
reported a total of 400 instances of involvement in a sexual
incident with an adult before they were 13. Exhibitionism,
fondling and manipulation of the girls' genitalia were the most
frequent experiences; only 31 of the 400 recalled experiences
included coitus or attempted coitus (Gagnon 1965). Despite
the considerable size of this sample it had, as Gagnon himself
pointed out, a general bias towards college educated women;
71 per cent of the subgroup who were questioned in depth having
been to college.

Another large scale study of university students 'primarily
from stable homes' was published by Landis (1956). Out of the
1,800 who completed questionnaires in the three year period of
research, 30 per cent of the men and 35 per cent of the women
reported some experience of an unacceptable sexual approach.
In the case of the women, the experiences were mostly at ages
below 15 and with males who were adult or considerably older
than themselves.

More recently Kutchinsky (1970), while carrying out a victim
study on 200 adult women in Denmark, found 14 (seven per cent)
who reported cases of 'indecency' as children and two (one per
cent) who had experienced incest. In Britain, few empirical
surveys covering child sexual abuse have been carried out.
Gittleson et al. (1978) interviewed 100 female nurses at a
psychiatric hospital in Sheffield and found that 34 per cent
reported that a man had exposed himself to them when they were
under 15. In Australia, Kapardis (1982) carried out a similar
study, collecting data by means of a questionnaire administered to 663 female undergraduates, of whom only 97 (15 per
cent) had been victims of indecent exposure when they were
girls under 15. Perhaps there is a genuinely greater incidence of exposure in Britain than in Australia; but nurses and
undergraduates may not be comparable groups.

The most comprehensive and the most recent empirical work on
child sexual abuse has been done in America by David Finkelhor
(1979). His main study was carried out on students of such
subjects as sociology, psychology, social work and human sexuality at six New England colleges. Sexual experience with
adults when they were children was reported by 19 per cent of
the 530 female and 8.6 per cent of the 266 male respondents.
The most common experiences were genital fondling (38 per cent

6

of female experiences and 35 per cent of male experiences) and exhibitionism (20 per cent of female and 14 per cent of male experiences).

In his latest works, Finkelhor (1982a and 1982b) reported the findings of an 'area probability' sample of adults in Boston. Of this more generally representative group, 12 per cent (521) reported sexual abuse as children (15 per cent of the women and six per cent of the men). This rate was lower than in his student population for two possible reasons:
(1)   the average age of the sample was older (median 38, and only eight per cent under 30), so their recall may have been less efficient; and
(2)   the sample included only adults who had children living with them. Therefore only adults who have been actively heterosexual were included in the study (although 66 of the 334 women were single parents).

In another retrospective study, using a sample from the general population, 28 per cent of female respondents reported some abusive sex experience when they were under 14 (Russell 1983).

Very little research of this kind has been done with British samples. In September 1982 a popular teenage magazine, '19', invited readers to fill in a self report questionnaire on their experiences of sexual abuse (Newman 1982). Over 3,000 readers replied and 36 per cent of these claimed that they had been victims of sexual abuse as children and adolescents (Newman 1983). That half of these were incestuous can probably be explained by the fact that the questionnaire and introduction were angled towards intrafamilial experiences, thereby possibly discouraging responses from those whose experiences were outside the family or who had no experiences to report.

Surveys of such self selective or otherwise unrepresentative samples, although useful in heightening the public's awareness of a previously neglected problem can lead to unjustified conclusions based on inflated incidence figures and a bias towards preferential reporting of the more serious types of abuse. This provides the press with opportunity for sensationalism. For example, an information pack prepared by the Scottish Women's Aid in 1983 alleged that 60 per cent of anorexia nervosa patients in an English hospital had been found to be incest victims; from which they concluded that anorexia nervosa might be considered a warning sign for incest. However, the study referred to was in fact no more than 'the early impressionistic findings of a research project

7

being carried out in Leicester' and not due for publication until 1985 (Buchanan 1983). The admirable intention of the women's aid group was to help women and children who are victims of sexual abuse, but that purpose would have been better served by surveying more representative samples. The present research was an attempt to take a first step towards this goal.

NOTES

[1] Sex crimes against children under 16 based on 1962 New York figures of 1,800 validated cases (Chaneles 1967).
[2] These were set up in 1973 and 1974 on the recommendation of the Department of Health and Social Security in order to supervise the management of nonaccidental injuries to children.

2 Design of the main study

The study was designed to obtain some indication of the extent and nature of girlhood sexual contacts with adults, to attempt to secure information about factors in childhood that might possibly be associated with these incidents, and to identify any long term effects attributed by adult women to such early experiences.

THE SAMPLES

It was decided to investigate only women because research sug- gests that young girls are more prone to sexual approaches than boys, and also because the predominance of homosexual molestations in the case of boys makes their experiences not properly comparable with those of girls (Finkelhor 1979, 1982a and 1982b, Landis 1956). It was felt that women generally find it easier to discuss sexual matters with another woman, and the interviews were all carried out by Ms Nash.

   Ideally, a prevalence study requires a random sample taken from a general population, but given practical limitations, the particular sensitivity of the subject matter, and also the need to select relatively young females, it was decided, as a compromise, to sample women from a G.P.'s list of registered patients. Several G.P.s were approached and all expressed interest in the project. Despite this, agreement to allow their patients to be approached was not forthcoming. Eventually, with the assistance of a university Department of Community Medicine, contact was made with one amenable G.P. As the senior partner in a large joint practice operating from two different health centres, his register proved to be particularly suitable. Of the 904 women, whose date of birth fell between 1943 and 1962 (i.e. aged 20 to 39) a random selection of 50 per cent was taken to produce our main target sample of 452.

A second sample of 148 female students was also invited to take part in the study in order to obtain results more comparable with the American data. They consisted of medical lecture audiences and women on the register of two colleges for graduate students.

METHOD

Potential respondents were approached by letter (see Appendix) from their G.P. emphasising his support for the project and the absolute confidentiality of information. Students were contacted via their colleges or at lectures. The women were invited to complete an anonymous self administered questionnaire and to supply a telephone number or address should they be willing to be interviewed. A combined reminder/thank you letter was sent three weeks after the initial contact. The content of the questionnaire (but not the fully spaced layout) is given in the Appendix. The questions were designed to be short, easily comprehensible and as inoffensive as possible. Questions on basic socio-demographic data appeared first, followed by those concerning childhood and early sexual knowledge as a lead-in to the sexual abuse questions. The questions were formulated so that for the most part respondents could tick categories rather than having to write out in full what might be embarrassing or disturbing particulars. One or two questions were open ended, such as 'How did you feel about what happened at the time?' and 'What was their reaction?'. The replies to these were classified later into roughly distinctive categories devised by the researcher. A space was left for respondents to comment on their reaction to the questionnaire.

Respondents willing to be interviewed were contacted to arrange a time and place convenient to them. Most preferred to talk at home when no one else was present. If the women were willing conversations were tape recorded for subsequent transcription. Even though nearly all agreed to this, many waited until the recorder was turned off before talking about some of their experiences. The length of the interview depended on how long it took a respondent to relax and feel comfortable with the interviewer, how many incidents she had to report, and how much detail she was willing to provide. The shortest interview lasted about 30 minutes (a respondent with no experience of sexual abuse in childhood or adulthood), and the longest approximately five hours. Respondents often digressed to topics peripheral to the main interview, but the semi-structured nature of the schedule allowed this to happen while ensuring that all vital questions were asked.

In the introductory letter, in the questionnaire and in talking with respondents the words 'contact' and 'experience' were used, in preference to 'child sexual abuse' or 'victimisation', as being more neutral and not anticipating what attitudes might be expressed. The term 'child sex abuse' is employed in writing this report merely because it is standard usage in the literature and conveniently short.

Where possible responses from both questionnaires and interviews were coded and put onto computer for analysis, using the Statistical Package for the Social Sciences (Nie et al. 1981). Transcripts were made of examples of different types of child sexual abuse and reactions to it. Other data were analysed by hand. For the purposes of the analysis, childhood experiences were defined as experiences occurring to a person under 16, and contact with an adult as contact with anyone at least five years older than the child in question.

3 Pilot work

In advance of the main study a draft questionnaire was tried
out on a small group of women to test its acceptability and
ease of completion. The terms used in the draft questionnaire
had been selected after preliminary testing on friends and
colleagues of the researcher. Only words that were readily
understandable and were in common usage were selected. Members of a parents' group in a distant city were chosen for the
pilot work, to ensure that nobody from the pilot study would
fall into the main sample. One of the leaders also ran a self
help group for women who had been victims of child sex abuse,
which ensured that counselling would be available should any
respondent become upset by the enquiry. This lady was also
helpful in encouraging members to reply and to agree to be
interviewed. The women were not necessarily themselves parents. They were told that the purpose of the pilot study was
to test our method of eliciting information. They proved very
helpful in subsequent discussions about the acceptability of
the wording and the sequence of questions. The design of the
final version of the questionnaire used in the main study (see
Appendix) benefited from this pilot work.

From 19 questionnaires sent out to the pilot group, 16 (84
per cent) were returned completed, of which 11 (69 per cent of
those returned) reported having experienced some form of sexual contact with adults as children. The lowest and highest
possible estimates of the prevalence of histories of child

12

sexual abuse in this group are therefore 11 of 19 (58 per cent) and 14 of 19 (74 per cent), according to whether none or all of those who did not respond are assumed to have had some experience.

The 11 women of the pilot group who reported some experience mentioned a total of 15 incidents (see Table 3.1).

Table 3.1
Experiences reported by the pilot group

Category of incident	Number of cases in category	Age(s) at time of occurrance(s)
Full intercourse	1	15
Attempted inter-course	4	5-10
Genital fondling	1	8
Sexual touching	2	12-14
Masturbating a man	1	8
'Propositioned'	2	11
Saw 'flashers'	3	7-12
Beaten for playing 'sex games'	1	4

One of the four cases of attempted sexual intercourse involved three separate occasions. One of the cases of 'sexual touching' consisted of repeated sexual hugging by a father, the other was leg stroking by a teacher. Three of the women reported further experiences as adults; one had since been raped by a stranger, another by her husband, and one had seen 'flashers' on two separate occasions.

As might be expected, lasting effects from early experiences appeared to be associated with the seriousness of the incident and the age at which it occurred. Thus, all those who had experienced attempted intercourse stated that they were still affected, as was the woman whose sexual organs were fondled at age eight and the woman who had been beaten for playing 'sexual games' at age four. Seeing an exhibitionist or being

13

propositioned apparently produced no lasting effects. The
woman who had experienced full intercourse at age 15 likewise
reported no lasting effects, but the adult in question had
been her boyfriend.

Besides providing advance information of the range of experiences likely to be found in the main study, the pilot work
also gave an indication of the probable response to requests
for interviews. Of the 16 women in the pilot group who returned questionnaires, eight declined subsequent interviews,
five of them because they had recalled no sexual contacts with
adults when they were children and felt that they had nothing
to contribute to research interviews. The three others who
did not want to be interviewed had all stated on their questionnaires that they were still affected by their experiences,
feeling 'sick, disgusted, angry', 'guilty and ashamed',
'angry', 'hurt', 'worthless', 'dirty', 'frightened', 'different', 'afraid of the future', 'sick about the past', 'unpro-
tected'. There was also a very real worry among those who had
had troubling experiences that others who lived with them
might find out.

4 Responses received in main study

Completed questionnaires were received from 223 of the 452 women in the sample from the G.P.'s list; 14 replied refusing cooperation and 31 letters were returned because the addressee had moved. The final response rate was thus 53 per cent of the 421 who received a request.

The student sample consisted of 148 women; of them, 92 responded, with four envelopes returned undelivered, giving a response rate of 64 per cent. (One hall of residence to which a large batch was sent had no system for retrieval of unreceived mail, so the true response rate was probably somewhat higher than 64 per cent). Finkelhor reported a higher response rate: 92 per cent from American students (1979) and 74 per cent from parents (1982a). His questionnaires to students were handed out and completed during class time, whereas our English students were contacted by letter or handed a questionnaire at the end of a lecture, leaving them to take the initiative in their own free time to complete and return the questionnaire.

The American parent group was contacted and interviewed in their own homes, the interviewer introducing the subject initially as a concern with the problems of 'raising a child'. This was doubtless more persuasive than our system of a mailed questionnaire with a covering letter which immediately introduced the subject of child sexual abuse. The doorstep approach may be acceptable in the USA, where people seem readier to communicate about sexual matters, but we felt unable to use it ourselves because it was thought too embarrassing and likely to be considered unethical. Moreover, we had no means of prior selection of house holders for age.

Given the nature of the present study and the method of approach, the response rate was as high as could be expected. Of the 223 responses received from the G.P. sample, 29 came in following the letter of reminder. In another study comparable to our own, which interviewed a random sample of 930 San Franciscan women, a response rate of only 50 per cent was achieved, despite paying each respondent $10 for her participation (Russell 1983), and in another survey, a short mailed questionnaire on sex stress yielded only 40 per cent returns (Goodwin, McCarty and DiVasto 1982).

Our questionnaire was designed to allow the more reticent to reply anonymously. However, no statistically significant differences were detected in the questionnaire data concerning childhood experiences between women who agreed to be interviewed and those who did not. Attempts were made to interview as many as practicable of the women who had reported some childhood incident and who were willing to be seen, and also to see a reasonable number of the women who had had no relevant experiences. A total of 109 women were seen, of whom 78 had had sexual experience with an adult as a child. A further eight women, who agreed to be interviewed, repeatedly failed to keep appointments and were not seen, although five of them had stated on their questionnaires that they had had sexual contact with an adult as a child. However, all five had also written either that they had never told anyone of their experiences before, or that they had been very upset by the incident. They probably had second thoughts when the time came to discuss it with someone. For example, one of them, who had been subjected to attempted intercourse twice at age six had written:

> The thing I can't understand about the incidents is why I did not tell my mother at the time (for that matter I wonder why I've never told her since) but I do remember that the man swore me to secrecy, I suppose I have always been good at keeping secrets.

In answer to 'How do you feel about it now?' another of these women wrote:

> Angry, for it did upset me deeply. The man was erect and I remember being terrified of men for a long while - really repulsed by their bodies. [She had been confronted by an exhibitionist when she was seven]

16

No significant differences were found between those respondents who replied after a letter of reminder and those who replied to the initial request. One of the women who responded only after a reminder explained:

> I sent the last questionnaire back blank as I didn't think what happened very important - I've filled it in this time and do not wish to take it any further. [She had seen a 'flasher' when she was eleven]

Reactions to the study and its subject matter were varied. One questionnaire was returned defaced. A few women complained that the enquiry was unjustified. For example:

> I am sorry, but your forms upset me and I am very surprised that my doctor sent me them, it is my business and not yours.

> I don't feel well enough at this time to answer the questions.

Others, however, volunteered more positive comments:

> The questionnaire is certainly essential. I certainly think that it is necessary for those who have experienced these sexual experiences to be able to talk to an unbiased outsider who is able to give advice and support.

Some respondents were obviously keen to cooperate. Four women who were in the process of moving house, although very busy, gave time to be interviewed because they felt the study to be important; so did three women with terminal cancer. Two others telephoned their G.P. to express their approval of his support for the project, although one or two others complained to him about it.

The number of responses and the number of incidents reported is shown diagrammatically in Figure 4.1. The 78 interviewed women who had some experience to report recounted a total of 138 incidents. The number of incidents reported by each woman ranged from one (the majority) to five (two cases).

The truthfulness of responses was impossible to test. Only the validity of statements of age could be checked against the G.P.'s register. There were no important discrepancies. In most cases the responses at interview tallied with those previously given on the questionnaire, except occasionally where a woman had initially minimised the extent of her experiences. In some extreme instances (four from the student group and 13 from the G.P. sample) respondents who had returned questionnaires signifying that they had had no relevant experiences actually described one or more during interviews.

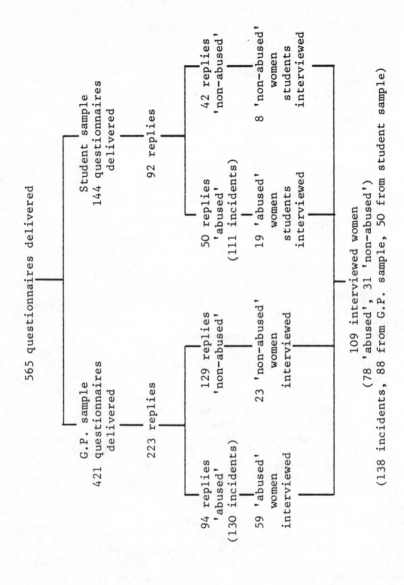

Figure 4.1 Responses received in the main study

565 questionnaires delivered

G.P. sample
421 questionnaires
delivered

223 replies

94 replies
'abused'
(130 incidents)

59 'abused'
women
interviewed

129 replies
'non-abused'

23 'non-abused'
women
interviewed

Student sample
144 questionnaires
delivered

92 replies

50 replies
'abused'
(111 incidents)

19 'abused'
women
students
interviewed

42 replies
'non-abused'

8 'non-abused'
women
students
interviewed

109 interviewed women
(78 'abused', 31 'non-abused')
(138 incidents, 88 from G.P. sample, 50 from student sample)

Questionnaires received from such women were recoded as positive for the purpose of more accurate analysis. Given that this could not be done for those who were not interviewed, the assessments of incidence from questionnaires are probably under estimates.

As in Finkelhor's work, we counted an incident as sexual whenever a respondent said that she had felt at the time, or realised afterwards, that what had happened (such as a hug or kiss) was sexual. Finkelhor (1979) believes that children perceive sexual overtures as such from a very early age:

> ...even very young children spontaneously recognised a sexual activity. (Obviously they did not understand "sexual" in the full sense that adults understand the term. But they knew the activity was different, it was taboo, it involved visceral sensations, and it should be done covertly or not mentioned). (pp.47-8)

Whilst one would agree with Finkelhor that a child will recognise an activity as 'different' (particularly if told to keep it secret) she may not always recognise its sexual connotation until, as an adult woman, retrospective recognition of its meaning may cause her to reinterpret it as 'sexual abuse'. Several interviewees said that although they were confused and frightened by a childhood experience at the time it was not until later that they understood what had happened to them:

Q. Did you know what was going on?

A. At the time I didn't. At the time I was too shocked to know that he was probably trying to rape me, but I knew that it wasn't very nice whatever he was trying to do.

Q. What sort of questions did he ask you?

A. The one I remember was "do you have a hairy fanny?" I didn't know what he meant.

(These examples, like all the quotations in this report, are as far as possible in the women's own words, taken from transcripts of tape recordings or written down at the interview).

Incidents which had made little impression when they were happening were sometimes claimed to have had long term effects. This justified our decision to include all experiences subsequently defined as sexual, even when they were recalled as having been merely unpleasant, confusing or simply amusing at the time.

5 Findings on the prevalence, frequency and type of early sexual experiences

PREVALENCE

Questionnaires describing some degree of sexual contact with an adult were received from 94 of the G.P. sample (42 per cent of those who replied) and 50 of the students (54 per cent of replies). This difference in the proportion claiming experiences was statistically significant (χ^2 = 4.26, p<0.05). Given that every one or none at all of the nonrespondents might have reported such an experience, in the G.P. sample the maximum possible prevalence was 69 per cent and the minimum possible 22 per cent. For the student group the maximum was 72 per cent and the minimum 35 per cent. The higher proportion reporting such experiences among the students may have been due to their being younger and thus having less far back to remember. The average age of the students was 26 (mode 24) whereas in the G.P. sample the average age was 30 (mode 36). Students may also have been less inhibited by the questionnaire approach.

The figures from our survey show a higher prevalence of recalled child sexual abuse than most previous studies (see Figure 5.1). However, if incidents not involving actual physical contacts are excluded, the results appear less diverse. Actual physical contacts between children and adults are reported by about one in six to one in four of women in most samples - including our own.

20

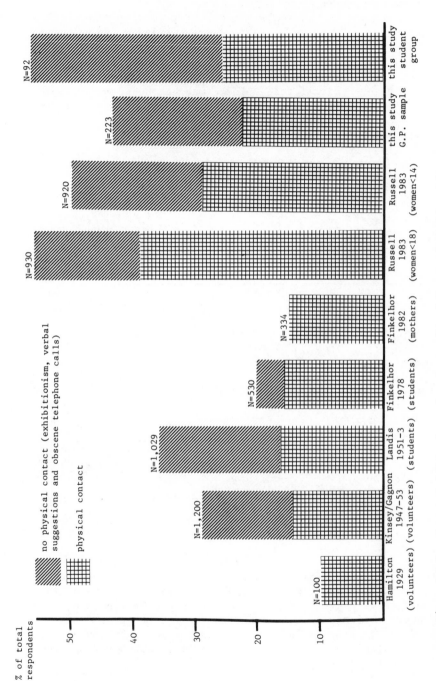

% of total
respondents

no physical contact (exhibitionism, verbal
suggestions and obscene telephone calls)

physical contact

Figure 5.1 Prevalence of childhood sexual contacts with adults as reported by adult women

TYPES OF EXPERIENCE

Sexual contacts between an adult and a child can take many
forms from a suggestion, to exposure, to fondling, to intercourse. The child can comply because she wants to, because
she normally submits to the authority of the adult, or because
she is frightened or forced. There may be one or more experiences, and each can be a single event, repeated, or built up
over time. The extent of girls' experiences reported on our
questionnaires is shown in Table 5.1.

Table 5.1
Extent of adult/child sexual contact
(percentages are of the total number
of women who completed a questionnaire)

	G.P. sample		Student group	
	No.	%	No.	%
No sex abuse	129	58	42	46
Single event	42	19	17	18
More than one event	21	9	18	20
Continued	12	5	11	12
Built up over time	6	3	–	–
Only discovered at interview	13	6	4	4
Total question-naires completed	223	–	92	–

It would appear from the table that the student group were
more likely to have a second sexual experience with an adult
or to have a continued experience. This may be a genuine difference, or it may have been due to the fact that students
(well used to filling in forms and explaining themselves in
writing) simply provided more information when they completed
their questionnaires.

Differences between the two samples also appeared in regard

to the type of sexual contacts experienced (see Table 5.2).

Table 5.2
Proportion of women experiencing certain types
of sexual contact with adults when they were children

Nature of sexual experience	G.P. sample (N=223)		Student group (N=92)	
	No.	%	No.	%
Verbal suggestion	14	6	13	14
Obscene 'phone call	4	2	7	8
Sexual kiss	21	9	15	16
'Flasher'	41	18	29	32
Adult fondled genitals	19	9	15	16
Adult caressed thighs, breasts	5	2	16	18
Attempted sex	8	4	4	4
Intercourse	4	2	3	3
Other e.g. made to touch adult's genitals, anal intercourse	14	6	9	10
Number of categories ticked	130	–	111	–

Students, whose recollections may have been more complete and more frankly expressed, reported having had more adult/child sexual experiences in every category. The differences were less marked for the more serious incidents, perhaps because these were less readily forgotten, and therefore recalled equally by both groups.

The age of girls at their first remembered sexual experience with an adult is shown for each sample in Table 5.3.

Table 5.3
Age at first remembered experience

Age in years	Questionnaires from G.P. sample	Questionnaires from Student sample
	Percentage of girls in each age group	Precentage of girls in each age group
0-5	5	4
6-8	12	24
9-11	33	22
12-13	22	24
14-15	28	26
	100%	100%

Overall there appears to be a gradual increase towards adolescence. The mean age at which all the reported sexual contacts with adults occurred in our sample was 11.6 years. The mean age for first remembered sexual contact with an adult was 11.3 years for the G.P. sample and 10.8 for the student group. This is slightly higher than that found in other studies: 10.2 (Finkelhor 1979), 10.4 (Landis 1956), 9.9 (Gagnon 1965). However, all studies agree that a large proportion of the girls who have sexual contact with adults do so at a very young age. Landis (1956) found 41.9 per cent of his female victims were under 11. This compares with 35.7 per cent in the present study. In Finkelhor's work 37 per cent of his victims were under ten.

One respondent in our study mentioned an incident at age three. It may well be that many very early incidents remain forgotten and unreported in retrospective studies such as this. Walmsley and White (1979) found that 3.2 per cent of their sample of female victims of sexual assault were under five years of age. Some of the very early cases cited by our respondents may have been remembered only because incidents continued to a later age, or because some later event prompted recall, as in the following example described by one of the women interviewed:

I have very vague memories of going to Germany on a train
when I was five. It must have been a troop train because
my father was in charge. We had a separate carriage, but
I slipped off - it was a long journey. There was a group
of soldiers in the corridor and they showed me something
like a darning mushroom. The soldiers laughed and I ran
off...I didn't feel threatened. I didn't bother telling
anyone. The very dim memory was awakened by my aunt's
darning...I was nine or ten, maybe older. My aunt was
there and my mother and my brother who was five. I saw
the darning mushroom and said "Oh, I saw a soldier with
one of those" and then it all came out.

Q. What was their reaction?

A. Surprise. "Good heavens". They played it very low key.

Q. How do you feel about it now?

A. It doesn't bother me. It's as though it happened to someone else - although I still remember it. I was lucky to
be very young and innocent at the time and therefore not
frightened as an older child might have been.

Mohr (1981) in his analysis of ages of Canadian children involved in paedophilic acts (from 36 clinical cases and 112
court cases) concluded that maximum risk was at seven to 11
years. However, in a survey of self declared British paedophiles it was found that they were most attracted to girls
aged eight to 11 with a 'minimum age of interest' around five
to six (O'Carroll 1980). The older girls' experiences in our
study may be attributable to the males involved being, not
paedophiles as such (the word means love of children) but men
who find adolescent girls particularly attractive and who
would not consider themselves deviants. The presence of teenage girls among prostitutes and strippers (and among some
brides of older men) indicates that many heterosexual males
must be attracted by this age group.

In order to ascertain how the women felt about the legality
of adolescent sexual experiences, those who were interviewed
were quizzed about their views on the legal age of consent to
sexual activity. The majority (particularly those who had had
no sexual contact with adults) felt that the present age of
consent (16) was still appropriate (students - 87.5 per cent
of those who reported no experiences and 58 per cent of those
who had reported some experience: G.P. sample - 67 per cent
and 58 per cent respectively). Where a change was considered
to be necessary, those who had reported experiences were more
likely to want the age of consent lowered (the youngest age
suggested was 13), whereas the others more often suggested it

25

should be raised (the oldest suggested age was 18). This result went against the expectation that women who had experienced molestation might develop stricter ideas on the age of consent. A few women thought that no law governing consensual sexual relations could be appropriate since girls attain physical and emotional maturity at different ages. A legal cutoff point, however, can act as a deterrent on occasion if the girl is aware of its existence. One respondent, who had been sexually propositioned by a man in her village when she was 15, said:

> It did not bother me. I simply told him I was under the age of consent and he just left it at that.

SEX AND AGE OF PERPETRATORS

As with previous research in the field, the vast majority of the adults who were sexually involved with the girls were male (Finkelhor 1979, 1982a and 1982b, Russell 1983, Baker 1983). In the present study only one female perpetrator was cited. She was an au pair engaged when the respondent was aged 13 to 14:

> It was about the time when I was pubescent. She was an au pair - Portuguese. When she was there first I felt as though she was my big sister (she was 24-ish) and we hugged and kissed and I later realised that the au pair reacted differently to other women who hug and kiss. I didn't know what was different. Then I learnt through school what a lesbian was and I thought Maria was...[The respondent later discovered this to be true]...I felt the pressure of her physical demands...Something about it frightened me very much and I became convinced she was trying to kill me.

If it is correct that fewer women than men develop a homosexual orientation, as Kinsey suggested, that might account for so few sexual contacts with female children apparently having a lesbian motivation. However, since convention permits love to be shown by females to children in their care by touch and cuddles, which are not usually intended by the adult or interpreted by the child as sexual, it may be that sexual motivation is more easily overlooked in their case. Men, in contrast, have usually been socialised into thinking of touch in a predominantly sexual context and may therefore experience more ambiguity and come more readily under suspicion when relating physically to children. In years to come this will probably hold less true since 'women's liberation' has allowed men to share in child care without feeling effeminate.

Previous studies have indicated that most adults who are sexually involved with children are in their thirties. Finkelhor (1979) gave the median age as 27.9 and De Francis (1967), in a study of victims known to the American Humane Association, as 31.3 years. In Baker's work in Britain the youngest perpetrator was found to be 14 and the oldest 70 with a mean of 32. The commonest age, however, was only 17 (1983).

One cannot expect an adult woman thinking back to a probably traumatic incident in childhood to remember accurately the age of someone many years her senior, especially as children often imagine adults to be much older than they are. With the possible exception of cases where the adult was a family member, our respondents' replies can only be taken as rough estimates. In 15 (11 per cent) of the cases of exposure respondents admitted that they could not give even an estimate since they had been unable to see the man's face at the time or simply could not remember. Those ages which could be estimated are plotted in Figure 5.2. The mean age was 35 years with a range from 11 to 80 and a maximum incidence in the late teens, the age at which Kinsey et al. (1949) found that males reach their maximum sexual activity. At this time of life, more than any other, some males may be open to any sexual possibility that presents itself, including contact with a child.

Mohr (1981) in his work on paedophilia concluded that there are really three phases of maximum risk. Adolescents (aged 15 to 19) may remain linked with children through their younger siblings, and may become sexually interested in these children if they have a lag in psychosexual maturation. The intermediate age group (aged 30 to 40) tend to have problems relating to other adults, and generally become involved with their own children or their children's friends. Mohr sees their involvement in terms of regression or substitution. In the older group (aged 55 to 59) opportunities for sexual activity or the capacity for it may have diminished and they often withdraw from social interaction, feeling more comfortable with children - sexually or otherwise. Our graph fails to show this clear trimodal pattern, but does bear out the observation that men sexually involved with children, unlike men who assault mature women, are often middle aged or older.

RELATIONSHIP BETWEEN OFFENDER AND CHILD

The relationship of the adult to the child at her first sexual encounter as reported in the questionnaires is shown in Table 5.4.

No. of adults/
incidents

N=138

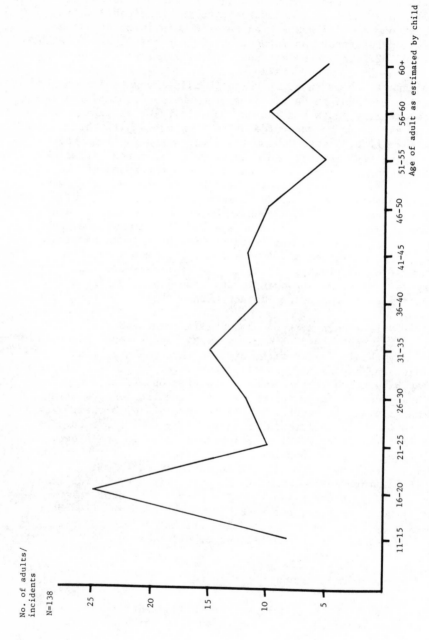

Figure 5.2 Estimated age of adults at time of sexual contact with child (interview data)

Table 5.4
Relationship of adult to child
at first remembered child/adult sexual contact

	G.P. sample (N=94)		Student group (N=50)	
	No.	%	No.	%
Father	3	4	–	–
Stepfather	4	5	1	2
Grandfather	–	–	2	5
Uncle	5	6	2	5
Brother/cousin	2	3	2	5
Authority figure e.g. teacher, G.P., vicar	3	4	–	–
Family friend	19	24	6	14
Stranger	38	49	29	67
Boyfriend	4	5	1	2
No information	16	–	7	–

Figure 5.3 sets out graphically the relationships involved in all the experiences reported by the interviewed women, some of whom had been involved with more than one category of perpetrator. It is immediately obvious that strangers, followed by family friends and neighbours, rather than family members, are most commonly cited as the adult partners. This seems to agree with earlier work such as Kinsey et al. (1953) in which 52 per cent of female respondents recalled the adult male as a stranger. Other researchers, however, state that the belief that most female child sexual abuse is perpetrated by strangers is erroneous (Mohr et al. 1964, Peters 1976). One reason for this disparity is that some investigators have counted only incidents in which physical sexual contact takes place (as in fondling or attempted coitus). In these cases the

29

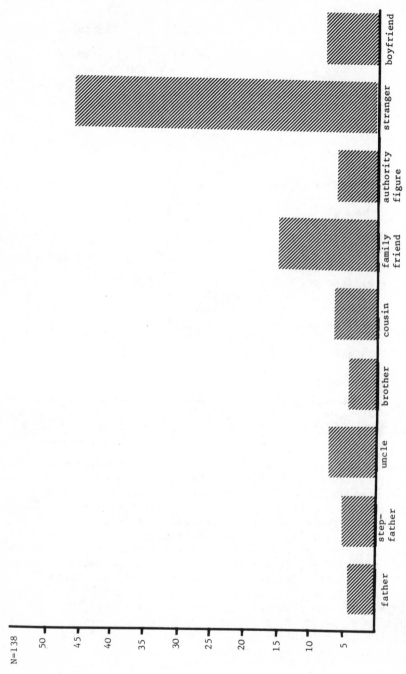

% of incidents

N=138

Figure 5.3 Relationship of adult to child at each sexual contact (interview data)

adult is more likely to be known to the child than where there is no physical contact (as in encounters with genital exposers).

6 The experiences described in detail

Unless otherwise stated the quotations in this section all come from the descriptions of 138 incidents given in the course of interviews with 78 women. The numbers and percentages derive from these totals.

VERBAL SUGGESTIONS

There were 13 instances of verbal sexual suggestions described by the interviewed women. Here is one example:

> It was outside the Catholic Church at the bus stop and a little old man started talking to me. I'd just been to church and Catholics say "be nice" so I talked to him...I got on the bus upstairs and he sat next to me. I asked for [name of local hospital] and he said "Are you a nurse?". I said "no" and he started being obscene... "Would you like to wash old me? What I'd like to do with a sponge...etc.". At first I kept saying "No no no, I'm not interested", then I shut up.

Q. How old were you at the time?

A. Fourteen. I'm sure blokes pick up girls like that because they know they can't cope with the situation. Basically you get in a situation and you feel stupid - you don't know what to do.

Q. About how old was he?

A. He must've been in his eighties - he could hardly get up
    the steps!

Q. What was your reaction at the time?

A. Very upset. I wondered should I scream - no one came to
    rescue me...I felt I couldn't get off early. I was trap-
    ped because he knew where I was going...He was repulsive.

Q. Did you feel responsible in any way for what happened?

A. No. I was shocked because I'd been pumped at school to be
    a good samaritan...I didn't talk to little old men again
    for a long time - I stayed well clear of them. I wanted
    to kick all little old men.

Q. Did you tell anyone about what happened?

A. My mother. She said why didn't you call the bus conduc-
    tor? She was very understanding and said it would be OK
    to call the bus conductor next time.

Q. How do you feel about it now?

A. I feel sorry for the little old men who came after and I'd
    been nasty to because of that. There must have been some-
    thing wrong with the man to do that to a young girl - he
    must have realised.

In five instances a verbal suggestion was the only sexual
approach by an adult that the respondent had experienced during childhood. The 13 incidents described occurred at a mean
age of ten (range seven to 15). Girls younger than this might
not have understood what was implied in verbal sexual overtures. Most of the males involved were in their mid-thirties
to mid-forties, but with a very wide range (13 to 80 years).
One was an uncle, one a foster brother, one a G.P., three were
persons known to the family and seven were strangers to the
child. None of the strangers was ever seen again. Those
known to the child tended to be avoided subsequently, except
for the foster brother, who was 24 years old and described as
'simple'. The incident had made the respondent more aware of
his vulnerability, so that afterwards she felt closer and more
protective towards him.

In four instances the male offered the child a bribe to make
sexual contact with him, but none complied, and only the foster brother repeated his 'invitation'. The majority of appro-
ches were made outside (seven), mostly on the street or in
parks. The child approached by her uncle, and the child whose
doctor made suggestions, were both on the adult's home ground
at the time. Usually the girl was alone (ten cases) but two

33

girls were with friends when the incident happened and one was with her sister. In this last instance the girls were walking by the beach in a resort town. Their faces were made up at the time and the man who suggested sex claimed that he thought they were prostitutes.

Generally, the girls were able to cope with these verbal suggestions and were little affected by them. As many were flattered and rather pleased by the attention they had received as were frightened (five of each). Three were repulsed by the approach. In only two cases was an actual attempt made to get away from the adult, although four women said they had realised at the time it was wrong. In the opinion of nine women the responsibility for the approach lay wholly with the man, but two were somewhat uncertain and two others believed that they might have encouraged the man by wearing mini-skirts. The fear that the clothes they wore might have provoked a man into sexual thoughts or actions was quite common (expressed by 16 of the 78 women who had had some childhood experience).

Of these 13 incidents only two were kept secret, in both cases because there was fear of being blamed for what had occurred. In most instances (seven) mothers were told and in two fathers were also informed. In the case of one of the youngest girls (aged seven or eight) the parents found out and their reaction occasioned her more distress than the incident itself. She had happily gone off with an unknown neighbour (whom she remembers as pleasant and friendly) to eat sweets at his home. Her playmates, however, more aware than she of possible dangers, told her parents who, in turn, informed a policeman friend. Her parents were, naturally enough, worried for her safety but in their anxious warnings gave her no comfort. The child ran to her room and cried alone:

> I cried and cried...He [the policeman] frightened the life out of me and I cried for ages.

Although unaffected by the event now, this respondent's reaction at the time, and those of others to be described in later sections, do bear out Reifen's fears (1957, 1958, 1973) that a child who has gone along happily with an apparently kind offender suffers distress and feelings of guilt only later, through the anxious or critical reactions of caring adults, be they parents or officials. In the one other case of verbal suggestion where the child had to talk to the police, she also said this was frightening and made her feel worse.

On the whole, the persons in whom the respondents confided these verbal encounters at the time do not appear to have been particularly helpful. Their most noticeable reaction was curiosity. In five cases the child was forbidden to go out under similar circumstances; in one case the reaction was described as 'didn't care'. Although five confidants expressed anger towards the perpetrator, one got angry with the child. In only four cases did the respondents feel comforted. Not surprisingly, few had told anyone since about the incident. One told her husband, one her children and one a female friend. The friend was amused, but the others were understanding and sympathetic.

Most of the women who had experienced sexual propositioning as children now felt indifferent about what happened, but three still felt some confusion as to what is normal between adults and children. Two said that their experience had made them wary of all men and one was afraid that similar experiences might befall her own children. Two expressed some degree of guilt, one pity and another anger and resentment for the adult involved. Looking back, two women wished that the police had been informed at the time, three believed that young girls should be taught to cope with sexual advances from older men, and two felt that nothing could be done because men are 'like that'.

OBSCENE TELEPHONE CALLS

An obscene telephone caller who is not seen by the victim, and yet makes contact within her own home, often when no one else is present, may appear more threatening to a child than a passing stranger who makes some sexual remark. Such was the case with the five interviewees who described this kind of incident in their childhood:

> I had just gone to live at my mother's. Someone rang and
> asked if my father was in...I said no and the man said
> "What's your name?". I said X and then everything was ad-
> dressed to X. He said "I bet you've got a nice body". I
> was shocked and put the 'phone down. I was alone in the
> house - it was about three in the afternoon...I was
> shocked, very upset and unnerved - I didn't think it
> would have such an effect...I felt awful because I'd told
> him my name...[I didn't tell my mother] because she
> would have had a neurotic fit...I was affected for a few
> days and didn't want to answer the 'phone...I've forgotten
> about it [now] but I wouldn't like to get another one.

The age of the respondents at the time of these telephone incidents ranged between 11 and 15, three were alone when the calls came, one was looking after a younger sister and one was with a baby-sitter. Two of the girls were frightened and

35

three shocked by what had happened.

> I slammed down the 'phone, ran round and locked all the
> doors and windows, took both dogs into the room with me,
> locked the door and sat with a dog at each foot and smo-
> ked. I think I was scared because we lived in the country
> and the nearest house was half a mile away and it was a
> sort of eerie type place.

The baby-sitter was told at once what had happened as were all
but one set of parents when they came home. Their reactions
were mostly comforting and they tended to play down what had
happened. The police were informed in one case, because the
calls continued over a month, but the girl did not have to
talk to them and so was not stressed. One incident concerned
a girl living with her mother, a singer, whose first name was
printed in the telephone directory. Several men called over a
prolonged period and the girl gradually became accustomed to
the calls and relatively immune to the obscenities. Looking
back on these obscene 'phone calls, only one woman remained
angry; the rest felt indifferent. Nevertheless, three did
mention that parents could help by instructing their children
how to deal with such calls.

EXHIBITIONISTS

Genital exposure was the commonest type of sexual behaviour to
which the interviewees remembered being subjected as children;
41 such incidents being recounted. Most were examples of the
typical 'flasher syndrome' - the man being in late middle age,
a stranger to the child and usually exposing his penis in a
relatively public place (14 on common land such as parks, ten
in the street, six whilst travelling by public transport,
three in school grounds and one in a cinema). Most (36) incidents occurred during the day or early evening, probably because this is the time of day when children are likely to be
out on their own. (During their later adult lives, 19 of the
interviewed women had been 'flashed at' on at least one occasion, but most often during the late evening). Girls 'flashed
at' tended to be post-pubertal; a half were 13 years old or
more (mean age 11). Exhibitionists, it seems, are less likely
to be genuine paedophiles than the perpetrators of some other
types of child/adult sexual abuse.

The vast majority of interviewees who had seen an exhibitionist in childhood had done so only once, although four who
had lived in London mentioned that seeing an exhibitionist had
been a frequent event throughout their childhood years. Few
of the women could recall with any degree of certainty whether

the penis was erect or flaccid or whether the man was masturbating at the time. Indeed some did not realise until afterwards that what they had seen was actually a penis, as in the
following rather typical case of an encounter one summer
evening, around seven p.m., experienced by a girl of seven:

We [the respondent and a female friend] were walking home
from a friend's in the park, along the bank of a river.
We heard footsteps behind and when we turned round there
was this scruffy man with egg on his suit. We started to
walk faster and he overtook us. My friend said "He's got
a sausage hanging out of his trousers". I said "What's he
got a sausage down there for?" and we ran past him for another look. He looked at us and grinned. Then my friend
said "That wasn't a sausage - that was a flasher" and we
ran home...I think we told my friend's mother and they
rang the police to make a complaint...It was rather funny.
I was shocked for a couple of hours - then we became mini-
celebrities at school. Our friends were amazed - it caused a sensation at school. Some friends wanted to know
all about it in detail and some set off for the park to
see if they could see him too...For the next few days we
all went around looking for a man with egg on his suit...
If it happened now I would report it immediately.

Despite the shock (mentioned in 18 cases) and the desire to
run away (mentioned in 16), respondents rarely remembered feeling threatened by the sight of a 'flasher'. The most commonly cited reaction was laughter or amusement. This was
particularly the case where the respondent was not alone. Indeed, being with peers seemed to protect the child from emotional trauma, as shown by some of the comments on feelings at
the time:

Shocked, then slightly frightened. I was with a school
friend at the time which lessened the impact somewhat.
[Age 13]

As there was four of us (all about the same age) we
thought it was quite funny. Had I been alone I think my
feelings may have been different. [Age nine]

In most of these cases mothers and/or girlfriends were told
of the experience. Friends generally giggled (with the respondent) about what happened. Parents tended to be angry with
the perpetrator and in 12 cases, including all the instances
where the exhibitionism took place in school grounds, the police were called. Generally the police proved to be helpful,
although in four cases the child found talking to them embarrassing, as in the following example of a girl who had been
really frightened by the incident:

37

I saw a flasher. He followed me when I was about 13...I
used to go up to a friend in the next village...I used to
go to collect the eggs, about 6.30, and this particular
night I saw this man on a motor bike and I thought it was
a bit strange and carried on going my way and he got off
his bike and started tooting...so I kept going and he followed me again and as I passed him and he came up and
asked me what the time was, but I was absolutely terrified
and then he shouted at me and when I turned round he was
there exposing himself. I was really terrified and that
day my friend happened to be late...Once he'd exposed himself he didn't pass me again. He was about 20. I didn't
recognise him because he was done up in his motor bike
gear. I had to talk to the police. They asked me to
identify a man they thought it was as he came out of a
shop. Well, I knew it was him, but I couldn't swear to it
in a court of law. He worked in the shop with my friend's
mother.

Q. What was your friend's parents' reaction?

A. Disbelief at first, in small villages it isn't often you
come across that kind of thing.

Q. What about your own parents?

A. They were angry, they were worried because I was frightened, but I think they were angry.

Q. How did you feel about talking to the police?

A. I felt dreadful, but the policeman he was really nice. So
understanding, but I was so embarrassed...

Q. What do you think helped you most at the time?

A. Certainly her parents and mine being so understanding and
the police being so understanding, but I was so embarrassed talking about that kind of thing to a man...I might
have been better talking to the policeman on my own and
not in front of my mum. I think it was worse talking in
front of all adults...I can remember thinking that I
couldn't go through with it. Feeling terrible and wanting
to crawl into a hole.

In ten cases of genital exposure no one was told about the
experience. One girl kept silent because she was afraid of
the police, others because they felt ashamed, did not wish to
embarrass their mothers, or were insufficiently troubled by
what had occurred. Looking back on these incidents of exhibitionism, indifference was the commonest feeling, mentioned by
22 adult women. A few (five) said that they had become wary
of all men after the incident. Nevertheless 'a mild amusement

and pity for the old guy' was the type of sentiment more commonly expressed (eight women). Seven believed that no effective action could ever be taken to prevent exhibitionism since
men are naturally so inclined.

Although most of the exhibitionistic incidents described
were minor isolated occurrences, six were of a more long term
and intrusive nature, lasting from one month to one year and
involving frequent self masturbation and obscene suggestions
by the male. The perpetrators in these more serious incidents
were 2 fathers, 1 stepfather, 1 brother, 1 family friend and 1
boyfriend. Due, no doubt, to their relationship with the adult, two of the girls felt trapped by the situation. One felt
increased affection for her father, because she considered
that his attention indicated that she was his special favourite. Except for the incident with the boyfriend, all these
encounters took place in their homes, and the girls felt at
least some fear. In two cases they were aware that what was
going on was wrong. Looking back, these women tended to feel
some anger and resentment about what had happened and were now
more aware of man's potential for such behaviour. The respondent whose brother used to masturbate in front of her when she
was aged ten to 13 described her current attitude as follows:

> Very frightened for other girls and women...It's so invas-
> ive seeing a chap wanking off in front of you when you're
> not even thinking of sexuality...I sometimes worry about
> it in the tubes - whether to be very cool about it and say
> "Is that all you have?" or whether just not to react in
> that sort of shocked way - that's what they get off on.
> Yes, I think I would report it - I think it's horrible and
> I feel that it's wrong - in our society and culture it's
> wrong and against women and it's very upsetting and can
> even be quite traumatic.

SEXUAL KISSING

Probably the least serious of the sexual incidents involving
bodily contact between adults and children concerned mouth to
mouth kissing, of which 17 examples were recounted to the interviewer. In nine cases the perpetrators used force and one
was under the influence of alcohol. In one case a stranger on
a train used actual violence towards the girl, but in all
other cases the adult was known to the child (5 family friends,
4 cousins, 3 uncles, 2 authority figures, 1 boyfriend and 1
relationship not stated). Most incidents took place in the
child's home (nine) or the adult's (four), often under the
pretence of kissing goodnight. The girl who was kissed by her
boyfriend felt closer to him afterwards, but otherwise either

39

the kisses made no difference to the relationship or else the men were generally avoided subsequently. Except for one seven year old, the girls involved were post-pubertal (mean age 12) and the adults tended to be relatively young (mean age 27).

Since the adults in question were usually known to the family, they enjoyed many opportunities to foist their attentions on the child. Indeed, in two cases the girl's parents were present at the time of the kissing. In two cases the kissing continued for over a year; few were solitary instances. In most cases (ten) the girls were shocked by the incidents, felt some degree of fear (three cases) or wanted to get out of the situation as quickly as possible (four cases). Only one felt indifferent to the actual kiss. Whilst five were physically repulsed by the mouth to mouth contact, an equal number experienced some pleasure and/or excitement from it.

Of all types of child sexual abuse, sexual kisses were least likely to be recounted to anyone else. Where a reason was given, most girls kept quiet because they were ashamed (two cases), because they didn't want to embarrass their parents, or because they were afraid that they would be blamed for having encouraged the behaviour (three cases). Interestingly, seven felt that they had indeed been to blame, in part at least, because of the clothes they were wearing at the time. One said: 'I knew I looked quite sweet in my pyjamas'. Of the three girls who reported what had happened, only one was able to say that her mother had comforted her. The parents of the other two girls did not credit their daughter's story or remained unconcerned, as in the following example:

I was about 13 or 14. I was very much in love with a rep [aged 45] who used to call round and he had been a friend of the family for years. He used to come and see us a lot and he came down one night and he had a fair bit to drink, and he kissed me goodnight. He kissed me lips to lips and stuck his tongue in my mouth and it was such a shock that I hated him for it. He held me so tight up against him and it was just such a shock. I didn't know what was happening. I didn't want to see him again, I hated him. I told mummy about it. I can't remember mummy being a lot of help to me then. I was terribly disgusted by it all and I didn't tell any of my friends. I felt horrible about it. Years later I confronted him about it and he said that he would never have done such a thing. I was about 18 then. I just thought it was better to tell him why I wouldn't speak to him for such a long time. He was such a handsome older man...and I felt really good with him when we went out with my dad and it was so awful to think that he had done that to me.

40

By the time of the interview, in most cases (13), the women concerned had come to terms with what had happened, but four women stated that their kissing experience, and the indifference of their parents to it, had rendered them somewhat confused as to what could be considered normal behaviour between a child and an adult.

NON-GENITAL FONDLING

Seventeen women who were interviewed described childhood incidents of non-genital fondling. The experiences and their effects were diverse, as in the two following examples:

I must have been about 13 or 14. He [the vicar] was about 50 to 60, somewhere around there. He just approached me and put both his hands on my breasts. That was in the courtyard, but it also happened in a passage near the vestry. It happened about three or four times. I was waiting for choir practice. I was always first there... because I don't like being late...I found it quite amusing ...I still laugh about it. He never felt threatening I suppose. I could deal with it by then. I said "You don't do things like that". He said nothing but got the message after the second time...Even now, when he's around here he's been like that with me and my daughter...he's just someone elderly who wanted a cuddle.

[My eldest brother] used to creep into my room during the night, and he would just put his hand on my chest, not my breasts, just my chest, and once he put his hand on my leg. I would wake up to find him in the room with me. It was as it he was sleep-walking and if I asked him what he was doing he would just walk out of the room, it was a strange thing but he did do it once in daylight. He was driving me back to school and he stopped the car and put his hand on my chest. I just told him to stop and then we had to stop to pick up a school friend of mine and so nothing more was said or done about it then...I mentioned it to a school friend and I mentioned it to a priest. I can't remember the friend's reaction; I think probably shock - but the priest was very helpful and told me that if it happened again I should tell my parents about it. But it didn't so I didn't...Perhaps he just wanted to find out what breasts were like or something. I just think he didn't know what he was doing. I didn't feel hate for him about it.

Q. What did you feel when it was happening to you?

A. Very confused and a bit scared, I suppose.

41

Q. What were you scared of?

A. The unknown I suppose since I didn't know what was happening. I can't have known much, if anything, about sex at the time [age 12]. I was only just developing at the time and I wasn't sexually aware of my own body, but I must have known something or I wouldn't have stopped him. I suppose I must have known it was wrong.

Q. Have you told anyone about it since?

A. I've told my husband and I've told my mother.

Q. What was their reaction?

A. My mother was fairly shocked, in that I didn't go to her about it at the time.

Q. You've only told her recently about it?

A. Yes.

Q. What about your husband?

A. Annoyed really, and sad for me. It has affected me sexually. It affected me and he was annoyed because of that. I think it made me afraid of sex.

Q. How do you feel about it now?

A. Confused about the way it happened, until [interviewer] said a lot of women's brothers have done this to them.

Q. Looking back is there anything that would have helped you at the time?

A. I don't know that telling mother would have helped me and I don't think she would have understood and I don't know what they would have done with my brother. I did feel better talking about it, particularly with the priest because I knew he would keep quiet. I don't think that anything could have been done at the time. I think if someone had sat down with me then and talked about sex it would have helped a lot.

Some of the characteristics of adult/child non-genital fondling were similar to that of sexual kissing - most of the 17 girls were post-pubertal (mean age 12) and force was mentioned in seven of the 17 cases, alcohol in one. The males involved tended to be a little older than in incidents of sexual kisses (mean age 31) and were more likely to be strangers. Of those known to the girl, 1 was a father, 1 a stepfather, 1 a brother, 2 were uncles, 1 was a family friend. Some of the offenders were authority figures (1 vicar, 2 teachers, 1 G.P.). One child was the willing partner of her boyfriend. When the fondling was by a stranger the incidents were isolated and took place in cinemas (two cases), on common land (two cases) or in the street (two cases) and during the daytime. However, as with sexual kissing, where the adult was known to the girl, the fondling usually took place repeatedly (perhaps continuing for a year or more) and either in her home (four cases) or on the adult's territory (three cases). Sometimes (four cases) other adults from the child's family would be present.

Reactions to what happened were shock (seven), fear (five) and attempts to avoid the man in future (six). Few told anyone of their experiences (only three told their mothers and three told friends), but two sets of parents found out what was going on. Mothers tended to comfort their daughters and express anger towards the adult, whilst friends were amused and curious. The commonest reason put forward for having kept the incident secret was because they were not troubled by it at the time (four cases). However, this may not be the only reason since three admitted that they had encouraged the man (passively if not actively), at least in part, and two said that they had derived some pleasure from the fondling. Indeed, one said that (at the time) she had been afraid that the police might take her away because of her participation.

The women's current feelings about these experiences seemed, in general, to be stronger than they had been at the time. Two women attributed their current sexual difficulties to these occurrences, three felt guilt and three regret about what had happened, six more were angry about what happened, two now bitterly resented the relative who had fondled them and five felt very wary of all men. As with those who had experienced sexual kissing, four of these women expressed confusion about what the sexual barriers should be between a girl and her adult relatives. Looking back, five said it would be helpful if parents or teachers were able to instruct girls in how to cope with such embarrassing and potentially disturbing incidents. Only two women expressed any pity for the man who had fondled them and believed that he needed some kind of social or psychological help.

GENITAL FONDLING

There were 21 interviewed women who had been involved in adult/child genital fondling (19 whose genitals had been fondled by an adult and two who had been forced to fondle a man's penis). Of these, six now felt completely indifferent to what had happened. Of those who believed themselves to still be affected, five remained wary of all men, three attributed their current emotional or sexual dysfunction to the abuse, one felt hatred for the adult involved, and two were left with some continuing feelings of guilt and disgust.

Remembered reactions at the time were varied, and generally related to the manner of approach and identity of the adult. Some girls had little idea of the man's intentions, as in the following cases, the first concerning a girl aged eight:

Well, he [brother five years older] took his clothes off and had a good look at me and I had a good look at him and he said shall we try doing this thing - which involved me lying down and him lying on top of me - and I said "What is this?"...I think I was a bit scared and that was about it - it all happened very quickly. Then he lay down on top of me and then he looked rather puzzled and I looked rather puzzled and that was it. Maybe we were interrupted, but I don't think so, I think we were alone in the house, and that was it...I knew I shouldn't tell my parents about it and I knew it was something secret.

...I'm trying to remember how old I was...about 12 or 13... I must have been about 13...I went to the [county] show on my own...and there was an Army demonstration...There was this army boy...he was showing me how to work this digger, and he had his hands on me and I didn't know what to do. I just carried on and we talked, but I can't remember what we said. And then we went behind the tents and he kissed me and undid my trousers...I just stood there...I hadn't a clue what he was on about. He said did I want to do any- thing, but I hadn't a clue what he meant then. [He was] 23 or 24, as I remember him now.

This second example appears relatively minor, in that the girl was post-pubertal, the age gap was relatively small (ten years), and the man was a stranger who attracted her 'for what he looked like'. Nevertheless, she still connected the inci- dent with her current inability to show affection within a sexual relationship. Perhaps there were more significant as- pects of what took place that she had blocked out or become unwilling to talk about. Alternatively, her current emotional problems may well have had other causes which she did not recognise.

In cases where the perpetrator was known to the child, the fondling was often accompanied by some degree of affection (four cases):

I was fondled by an adult [family friend]. I used to go to their house, they had no children...and he would take me on his knee...and he would just stroke my leg and ease his fingers into my knickers. He never did anything that

hurt or that was remotely unpleasant. I think [I was] between seven and eight. He would be in the late forties.
I knew all along that this was wrong...I just knew that it
was wrong and I felt awkward about it. It was sort of
dirty. It would be in the afternoon after he came home
from work. [It was] neither pleasant nor unpleasant. I
stopped going after a while, quite deliberately. I knew
it was wrong at the time, but as I got older it became
more serious.

Q. Did you tell anyone about it?

A. No, not ever till I answered your questionnaire.

Q. How do you feel about it now?

A. I am very glad that there wasn't a great blow-up about it
...The way it went it didn't become a serious thing, it
was just a small incident that I was able to deal with
without any trouble really and it just went away. There
was no trauma. Had other people got to know then there
would have been a lot of trauma.

In some cases the child felt unable to extricate herself:

He [cousin] must have been 11 or 12 years older than me.
I remember pedalling round to see his stamp album of all
things. I can remember him having cold hands and him putting his hands up my legs. I knew it was wrong and I was
so embarrassed, but I couldn't think how to tell him. I
didn't know what to do. Then his mum came upstairs and he
took his hand away. I must have been about 11. I remember knowing that it was all wrong, but I didn't know how
to handle it. I remember being very hot and bothered and
sweating. It was more embarrassment more than anything
else...I used to collect stamps and he collected stamps.
I don't know whose idea it was - it could have been my
aunt or my mother's. I was totally innocent at the start
of it and I was totally shocked when he put his hand up.

Q. Did he say anything?

A. Not a word. He asked me to look at his stamps.

Q. With his hand still there?

A. Yes, it sounds so stupid really, he was fiddling about. I
didn't think his hand was warm enough. It was just simply
that I didn't know how to handle it, the situation. I
didn't know how to get rid of him. It was a bit of a
shock because at that age he had always struck me as being
sane and sensible. It is just one of those situations
where he had said how cold his hands were and then stuck
his hand up between my legs and said "You're nice and warm

45

in here, I'll warm my hands in here". I don't think there is any other answer other than I should have told him to put them on a radiator.

Force or violence was involved in six cases. Where the perpetrator was a stranger, the fondling would probably be better described as grabbing, as in the case where a nine year old girl was tied to a tree, stripped and 'fingered and fiddled about with' by a group of teenage boys. She was too frightened and upset to tell her parents and remembered being terrified, unable to sleep for ages, and crying nightly for weeks. She said she still had nightmares about what happened, believed she was 'still affected to this day', and 'doesn't trust men'. Indeed, she was shaking with anger and emotion as she recounted her story.

In the six instances where force was used the girl tended to be shocked and frightened. The two girls who had masturbated the male felt repulsed by what happened. Three women claimed to have blocked out their reaction, at least in part, possibly because the memory was too painful (one woman did recall actual physical pain) or maybe they had repressed it because the experience had been sexually arousing (four women actually said that they had experienced pleasure from the fondling and believed that they must therefore have encouraged the adult in some way). Here are two more (non-violent) examples:

I could have been about nine or ten, something like that. [He was] an older man, he was doing something in the rec. and we used to go into his caravan, just innocently. He was about 30...his name was [X] and there were two or three of us and the other two went and I was left there talking...I really can't remember the details. I know he started with his hands and I can't remember whether he took my pants down. He was just doing it gradually while talking. I don't know how I got away.

It was a next door neighbour. I think he must have been about 18. He didn't actually live there, he was a friend of the family. He used to give me sweets and chewing gum, things that I'd never sort of seen before and there was a passage near the house and he'd want me to touch him and put his penis between my legs and that, but he didn't actually enter as far as I can remember. It didn't strike me as wrong as far as I can remember, perhaps because somebody of five doesn't think things are wrong like that, but what I can't forgive myself for is that I didn't think it was wrong...I mean he wasn't forceful or brutal or anything. I didn't find it repulsive or anything...perhaps children of five today would. I just sort of fondled him

46

and he used to put his penis between my legs. But he never entered. Knowing what I know now it was wrong, but I didn't think so at the time. Why didn't I say something to my mother?...I can't work that piece out. He didn't hurt me or threaten me or hit me or anything like that. Perhaps I would have been more frightened if he had...I wasn't frightened I know that.

Q.   He didn't ejaculate or anything?

A.   I can't remember but it would have been more frightening if he had.

Q.   Do you remember if his penis was erect or not?

A.   No, I can't remember. I can remember it being warm.

Q.   Did you tell anyone?

A.   No, someone saw us and told someone.

Q.   Can you remember your mother's reaction?

A.   Upset, crying, I should think she told my grandmother. I thought I'd done something dreadfully wrong. She [mother] just said "don't let boys do that to you". I can't remember her telling me how babies were made or that it was wrong. I remember we went to the doctor's and I had an examination. I was still a virgin...I was a bit worried and frightened...I couldn't make out what was happening then to have to go to the doctor because of this...I [felt] worse about going to the doctor really. I can't think why I didn't think it was wrong, why I didn't tell my mother sooner. I think the doctor was what worried me and I thought that there was something wrong with me. It was that that worried me, without the fuss I think it would have just passed over.

In the last quotation, it is interesting to note once again that it was the parental reaction and examination by a doctor which upset the child more than what had occurred with the youth.

In over half of the incidents (13) the respondents told no one of what had occurred, although three of these were subsequently discovered. Mostly the girls had felt they would be blamed for what had happened (four cases), and it would embarrass their parents (two cases) or that the police would take them away (one case). In only three cases did parents who knew what had happened to their daughter comfort her. The reactions of others were less helpful: two were angry with the adult and one with the child, whilst one was shocked and three forbade the girl to get herself into such a situation again.

47

Women who reported genital fondling during childhood tended to remember it as having occurred at a relatively young age, 15 out of the 21 being under 13 (mean ten years). Somewhat surprisingly, the perpetrators in seven instances were almost strangers to the child. Those better known to the girls were family friends (six), stepfathers (three), cousins (two), uncle (one), boyfriend (one) and teacher (one).

The adults involved tended to be quite young; 12 were estimated as being under 40 (range 18 to 60). Many (ten) instances of genital fondling were single occurrences, but where close relatives were involved and the abuse took place at home, it sometimes continued for a year or more (four cases). One respondent said she had been subjected to repeated genital groping from various males when she was a young girl travelling on the London underground.

INTERCOURSE AND ATTEMPTED INTERCOURSE

Twelve cases of intercourse and an equal number of cases of attempted intercourse were recounted by interviewees. As one might expect, memories of such events tended to remain vivid. Only one of those who had experienced attempted intercourse and one who had had full intercourse as children said that they remembered feeling indifferent to it at the time. Even here, the interviewer had the impression that the respondents were too embarrassed or otherwise unwilling to remember or to disclose fully their feelings. However, where the adult involved in full intercourse was a boyfriend (five cases) the girls tended to experience less emotional trauma at the time and to be relatively untroubled by it later. In three of these cases the women said that they had actually encouraged the man to have intercourse with her and four remembered the experience as pleasant. In none of these five cases did the women define the experience as abusive in any way:

> I lost my virginity at 13 and he was about 18 but I didn't think that I had been abused by an adult...I was extremely innocent about sex and I got involved with someone on holiday and it just happened. I think I looked old for my age. I was with my sister and brother and then there were some older girls who I became involved with. I think they were about 17. We went to the local disco and met some people there and the four of us went out one night and went back to one of the boy's places. I didn't know exactly what was happening, but my friend was going off to another room with her friend and...I think he suggested it but I was completely willing...The next day I was very frightened because I saw that I had been bleeding, and I

thought something terrible must have happened. I saw him
several times after that and [intercourse took place] half
a dozen times. It wasn't until we got back to England
that I started feeling terribly guilty about it...At the
time I enjoyed it. I don't regret it at all. The only
doubts I do have now is that it can make your partner feel
inadequate if you have had more experience and that can
make difficulties...I would do the same [again].

In the next example the boyfriend's advances had been rejected,
and although full intercourse did not take place feelings were
more negative:

He got a bit nasty with me one night and he tried to have
sex with me...I wanted to kiss and cuddle with him and I
liked him very much. He was about 27 and he put his arm
through the greenhouse window and that stopped him from
what he was doing. I suppose it was my fault for letting
him kiss and cuddle me, and it was outside in the garden,
but when he tried to lift my skirt and pull my knickers
down, I started panicking and pushing him away. I had to
tell mummy because she would find the glass broken, and I
told her about it. Afterwards I thought he was a creep.
I didn't see what gave him the right to get so pushy when
I said no to him...he undid his trousers to show it
[erect] to me. He tried to grab my hand and put it on it.
I pulled away, I felt sick and I thought it was horrible.
[This girl went on to have full intercourse a few months
later with an 18 year old]

More serious were the cases in which the adult was not a boyfriend but a relative (3 fathers, 1 stepfather, 3 older brothers, 2 uncles, 1 cousin), a family friend (five cases) or a
stranger (two cases). In fact ten of these cases involved
force or violence and another threatened violence. Moreover,
of all the experiences recounted, these were the ones most
likely to start at a very early age (some at three or four)
and lead up to full intercourse gradually. In fact ten of
these episodes continued over a year or more. Excluding the
cases of boyfriends, the mean age for attempted intercourse
was eight and a half years, and for full intercourse ten
years. Full penetration rarely took place very much younger
than ten. A striking exception was the respondent who, at
four years of age, was penetrated by a childless neighbour and
then left bleeding on her parents' doorstep.

The younger the child, the less likely she was to understand
what was happening:

I'm not sure whether he was trying to have sex or whether
he was just using me for masturbation...It was a young man

49

who used to work for my father, he must have been about 17.
He had appalling boils on the back of his neck. He used
to hide in the farmyard and catch me as I was going by and
first of all he twisted my arm up my back and made me pro-
mise not to tell anybody. He would take me to the hay
shed, where there were bales of hay and to begin with he
just used to rub himself up against me fully dressed. As
time went on, he used to take down my knickers and make me
lie on my back and he would lie on top of me and he'd make
me feel his penis and he'd have orgasms on top of me. I
don't think he ever tried to achieve penetration or anything like that. He may have done, because as time went
on more and more happened. He was getting me completely
undressed and my sister as well. I remember it happening
when my sister was three or four and I would be six or
seven. It went on for quite a long time...I would go in
to the house and clean myself up...I usually had straw in
my knickers. I used to do my best to avoid him but I
couldn't stay indoors all the time. I thought it was all
pretty unpleasant...It may have happened 20 or 30 times.

The following example illustrates a similar lack of understanding. The victim was an educationally subnormal girl sent
by her mother to live with a middle aged male friend when she
was 15:

The first time he told me to lay on the floor - I did and
he started doing things - he didn't give me a chance to
get away or say no. He took his clothes off and told me
to take mine off. He got hold of me and had sex with me.
I was scared - it was horrible. When I went to the toilet
it hurt - I shut myself inside for two or three hours. It
felt horrible...He hurt me. I was frightened he might do
it again if I told anybody. [Nevertheless, this girl subsequently rang her social worker and was taken away from
the man]

The male perpetrators (even when boyfriends and brothers are
excluded from calculations) were not particularly old (mean
age 39, range 20 to 58). In cases where the adult was a relative the child would generally try to avoid him in future (six
cases). At the time, two girls felt hatred for, and seven
fear of, the man who had obtained or attempted intercourse.
The overriding memory of those who had been penetrated was of
physical pain. Although at the time the girls who were involved with relatives or who experienced full penetration believed that they were not to blame, usually they were too
frightened to tell their mother about it, often because the
perpetrator had threatened dire consequences if she did not
keep the secret:

It was my uncle who was blind. He's dead now. It's an
awful thing to say but I'm glad he's dead. He died of
leukaemia. Every week they used to ask us there for tea.
I can always remember being frightened of him even when I
was small. He was always (I don't know whether you have
ever known a blind person but they always feel you anyway)
he was always like this to everybody and I can remember my
parents and all the relations joking with him and saying
"oh you dirty old man". He always used to make some ex-
cuse and he always told them to take the boys out into the
garden or take them out shopping and buy them sweets and
it just used to start like that. Oh, here I go again,
[respondent upset] I get some sort of block...I can remember him breathing, like a dirty old man and I can remember
him putting his arm around me and he would always be doing
that and, one day, he asked me to go into the hall with
him and he got me in the corner and he pushed me, and I
can remember him pushing me up against the wall and
breathing heavily and him saying things like "You'll like
it really, everybody does it, even your mum does it, but
she doesn't tell anyone, you mustn't tell anyone about it
because it's rude". All the while he would be putting his
hands up my skirt. It was awful. I used to stop him, but
being the size he was he was stronger than me and I used
to dread going round there, but he used to get quite violent. He hit me once, he didn't hit me a lot. He used to
frighten me so much. When you're that age - he used to
say that if my mum and dad thought I was being nasty to
him they would tell me off and hit me. He said "They'll
send you away to a home" and being that age, well you believe it all...I can't really say it affected me, you hear
some people say it ruined their lives and they don't like
sex and don't even want to get married. I suppose I'm
strong. I used to fight him off and scream and yell to
get him off. I makes me sick to talk about it, I'm shaking even now just talking about it and it's a nasty thing
to have happened. When I talk about it and I can feel my
tummy turning over and I thought one of these days he
would kill me. I thought he would kill me. I thought he
might strangle me. He used to say he'd take me away or
he'd tell my mum that I'd been a naughty girl. I thought
it was me who was wrong at the time I thought everyone did
it and that it was just me...He used to kiss me, I used to
turn my head away, I still cringe to think about it. He
used to dribble anyway, it still makes me feel sick, anyone dribbling, I suppose anybody feels the same. He used
to try to have sex, he used to grab hold of me, but I always managed to stop him. I think he would have had sex
if he had had the chance. He used to take his whatsit out

51

and I wouldn't look and he used to ask if I had seen one
before. I said I'd seen my little brother's and I didn't
like that so I knew I wouldn't like his. I think [it was
erect] because I remember feeling it [on her chest because
he was so much bigger] and it's embarrassing really isn't
it, but it must have been...I think if I had known [things
like that sometimes happen to children] I would have told
my mum and dad and I would have known that it was wrong.
I knew about little kids getting killed, but I never knew
those sorts of things happened to them.

In five cases one of the child's parents discovered what was
happening. The police were called in two of these cases and
in another the girl was taken to the doctor. Although these
authority figures were generally felt to be 'helpful', the
girls did not really understand at the time what was the nature of their involvement, and tended to feel that it was
their fault that a fuss had been caused.

Of the 24 women who had experienced attempted or completed
intercourse as children, including those whose contacts had
been with boyfriends, only six could look back on their encounters with equanimity. Their currently expressed sentiments included hatred for the man (five), guilt and disgust
about what had happened (five), sexual and emotional difficulties attributed to the abuse (three), wariness of all men
(two), fear for other children (one) and confusion (two).

SEXUAL CONTACT WITH FATHERS AND BROTHERS

Although the intrafamilial relationships have already been included in previous sections, it is thought useful to examine
them further, since many books have been written on this subject alone (Weinberg 1955, Maisch 1973, Meiselman 1978,
Justice and Justice 1979, Forward and Buck 1981, Herman 1981,
Goodwin 1982, De Young 1982, Renvoize 1982, Nelson 1982). As
Finkelhor (1979) discovered, sexual contacts by fathers with
their female children rarely involve actual intercourse. However, Renvoize (1982) points out that sexual acts other than
intercourse can be just as traumatic. In our interview sample
only one father actually penetrated his child. One older
brother also did so. Two brothers attempted intercourse, as
did one natural father and one stepfather. Fondling and masturbation were more common. The reported incidence of sexual
contact with father and brother in the present study is compared with the findings of Finkelhor (1979) and Russell (1983)
in Table 6.1.

52

Table 6.1

Childhood sexual contact with fathers and brothers
as reported by adult women

	Finkelhor		Russell[a]		Present study			
					Questionnaire data[b]		Interview data[c]	
	(N=530)		(N=930)		(N=315)		(N=101)	
	%	No.	%	No.	%	No.	No.	
Biological father	0.9	(5)	2.9	(27)	1.0	(3)	(5)	
Stepfather or father figure	0.4	(2)	1.8	(17)	1.6	(5)	(7)	
Brother[d]	13.6	(72)	2.2	(20)	1.0	(3)	(5)	

Notes

a. In Russell's study the cutoff age for childhood was 18 years – a possible reason for higher percentages.

b. N.B. Not all respondents identified a perpetrator on the questionnaire, hence the numbers under-estimate the actual prevalence.

c. Percentages are not shown in this column because they would be inflated by the fact that a greater proportion of women who had experienced child sexual abuse agreed to be interviewed than did those with no such experience. More instances appear under this column because some women had not given the identity of the adult in their replies to the questionnaire.

d. Finkelhor fails to define the age difference between the siblings – a possible reason for this high percentage. In the present study any sexual games between siblings with an age gap of less than five years were excluded.

It has been suggested that,

> incest is likely to happen when traditional beliefs about
> the roles of the husband, wife and daughter are taken to
> extremes: when family members are seen as the husband's
> property, and sex is among the services they are expected
> to provide. (Nelson 1982, pp.10-11).

The findings of a self report study might well not reproduce
observations drawn from cases reported to the authorities.
However, it was noticeable in our sample that paternal sexual
abuse did tend to take place in families where the man was
dominant and quarrelled frequently with his wife. In none of
the cases involving a father or stepfather did the victim recall her parents being affectionate to each other in her presence. Justice and Justice (1979) have described the
incestuous father as jealous and tyrannical in an over protective way. One small study of 14 American incest cases found
typical fathers (or stepfathers) to be violent and mothers
chronically depressed (Browning and Boatman 1977). Although
the incestuous fathers (or stepfathers) in our interview sample were generally considered by their daughters to be author-
itarian and might hit the girls as a means of discipline, they
were not described as brutes and they would use 'affection'
rather than force at times of sexual contact. This is probably typical of the many cases that do not get reported to the
authorities. Obviously, when actual intercourse was attempted
or achieved, pain was caused due to the disparity in size of
the sexual organs. It was at this stage that the girls tended
to become frightened and begin to realise that something was
'wrong' in their relationship.

> I don't know how to put it into words to tell you. I
> didn't understand or feel I was doing anything wrong.
> When mum was out my stepfather would lock the door to the
> front room. Then he'd sit me on his knee and talk to me
> and touch me. I wasn't too bothered at the time, I was
> very immature and hadn't been told about the facts of life
> at the time [aged ten]...He would touch me and want me to
> touch him, and I did because I didn't know I was doing
> anything wrong. Then he tried to have sexual intercourse.
> He didn't get very far. That frightened me. [After three
> or four attempts at intercourse, this girl told her
> mother, although the fondling had been going on for six or
> seven months previously]

Unless actual penetration was attempted, sexual contact tended to be accepted simply because young children usually obey
their parents without question:

> I was frightened...but when it's your father you don't

know whether or not it's wrong. I didn't feel it was
right, but because it was my father I thought perhaps
maybe it was all right.

It has been suggested that a high percentage of incestuous
fathers are chronic alcoholics (Maisch 1979, Virkunnen 1974,
Renvoize 1982, Lukianowicz 1972). The reason given is that
alcohol may reduce a man's self control and permit the acting
out of desires which would otherwise be suppressed. In the
present study, alcohol was found to be involved in only one
case and even then it was used to disinhibit the child rather
than the adult.

Obviously, if the father is unemployed (as in one case of a
stepfather in our study) or the mother is absent from the home
(as in one case of a natural father in our study) there is
more opportunity for incest to take place (Weinberg 1955,
Lukianowicz 1972, Renvoize 1982). However, even when such
evident opportunity did not exist, the offending fathers in
the present study were not deterred from visiting their daughters in their beds whilst other members of the family slept
nearby:

> My dad just used to come in when I was in bed. You know
> when I was asleep. Half the time I used to make out I was
> asleep. It used to be in the middle of the night...He
> used to get in bed with me. He used to have it with me, I
> never thought...I used to think it was natural until I was
> 13 or 14, I didn't realise how serious it was. I thought
> every father...I thought they did it to all the daughters.
> You know, I had a couple of friends at school and you know,
> you talk with other girls, and I thought there was some-
> thing wrong with their dads that they didn't do it to them.
> It was my dad that was wrong. I was just coming up to my
> eleventh birthday, before full intercourse took place, be-
> cause he called it a birthday present. Some birthday
> present. It wasn't until he had started to see that I was
> growing up.

Q. When he started doing this to you, did you feel differ-
    ently towards him?

A. Yes, I loved him more, but only because I thought it was
    his way of showing that he loved me, in the normal way.

Q. Was there ever anyone else around?

A. My sister used to be asleep in the next bed.

Q. Did he approach her in any way?

A. No, he didn't.

Q. How long did it go on for?

A. Until I was just 14.

Q. Do you remember how it stopped?

A. I used to put a chair up against the door when we went to bed at night, and every time he came near me I just moved away. I started to realise that it was wrong. I didn't know how to go about telling anyone. He used to try to get in. He said something to me and I told him I didn't want him touching me no more. For a few weeks he didn't speak to me at all, and then he just carried on after that as if nothing had ever happened.

In the above case the father stopped when the girl asked him to do so. Other fathers were not always so easily disuaded. One girl, who had enjoyed her stepfather's attentions (fondling) between the ages of 13 and 14, because she found them erotic and because it made her feel 'very special because of the power of knowing someone wants you', changed her attitude when she was eventually found in bed with him by her mother and sister. They both thought it 'very odd' and she felt devastated by the discovery. In later contacts she tried to make her stepfather 'realise what he was doing', but with little success. Once he saw that she had begun to reject him, he became aggressive towards her (and towards her younger sister) and would especially try to rub himself against her if her mother was around because 'he seemed to get a kick out of it if mum saw'.

Maisch (1973) quotes the onset age for incest victims as between 13 and 15. The present study found the earliest age of onset of intrafamilial contacts to be only three years old (mean age ten and a half). However, the youngest age at which actual penetration took place was nine, and that was by an elder brother. As Renvoize (1982) suggests, girls at such an early age may have no idea what is happening to them. In the following case the mother also appears to have been in a state of ignorance:

I think we were playing hide and seek, something like that. I know I went home and I was bleeding and she [mother] thought I'd had an accident, and I never told her what really happened. She just put it down to an early period. I didn't really understand. It hurt, but I never really understood.

Two years later this girl was raped by her father also, but again did not tell her mother because 'I thought I would have been blamed for encouraging it or something'. A similar

reason was given for keeping silent in most cases of father/
daughter contacts, particularly where the girl's relationship
with her mother was difficult, as in the following case:

This is the bit where I get stuck. It was my father. I
would wake up, I always used to sleep in pyjamas and my
father would be rubbing his penis against me. I think I
was around 13 or 14. Of course I was petrified and I sort
of rolled over, turned away and I was really frightened
and I didn't know what to do. I thought, well, if I tell
my mother, I don't think she'd believe me. I just didn't
know what to do. It really did scare me witless and I
just didn't know what to do. I screamed and moved as if I
had just been woken up and frightened. I rolled over and
curled up in a corner. This went on for ages and I just
was very frightened. I knew it was wrong, but I didn't
know what to do, and I wouldn't tell my mother. I didn't
think she would believe me. I mean we didn't get on in
any case and I thought that if she thought my father was
creeping into my bedroom, it would be even worse. When I
was 15 my mother went into hospital to have a hysterectomy
and she was very ill and my father looked after us. My
father worked away and the weekend she went away he came
back...I was scared to go to bed at night, my mother not
being there. We were drinking ginger beer at home and my
mistake was whisky. I was sick and I went and made myself
sick. Since I grew up I knew the taste was whisky. I
hadn't realised at the time, I was given this glass and I
drank it and I felt very whoosey and I was sick and I went
to bed and my father tried to have sex with me. I really
did scream, my mother not being there I really did scream
blue murder and I made my brother come in and sleep with
me and closed the door. I think I said that daddy was
drunk or something. So I tried to hide from him as well
as I could, but he knew I was terrified...We pulled the
chest of drawers across the door and I wouldn't come out
of the room all the next day and he was off to work on
Monday. We barricaded the room so he couldn't come in. I
just couldn't tell my mother. We were always arguing and
I just didn't think she would believe me. She would have
said that I had egged him on or something, because I was
tall and I think I had a good figure for my age, my mother
being very short and very fat. My mother came home and I
was in a terrible state. I wanted to be out as much as I
could be and when my father was about I couldn't stand to
be in. I just didn't want to be there when he was there.
I used to go upstairs to do my homework...He wasn't home a
lot. I was lucky. I didn't see much of him. I think if
my mother had known the reason it would have been better.
Even now I couldn't let her know the reason. We get on OK

57

now that I'm older.

Q. Apart from your feelings of terror, did it have any physical effects?

A. I used to feel aroused...but it was a feeling I couldn't understand, I know now what it was, but I didn't then. It was a feeling I honestly didn't understand, but now, it was a fact that I had been aroused.

Q. Did you find it at all pleasurable?

A. No, definitely not then, I was absolutely terrified.

As can be seen from an earlier quotation, one girl told her school friends about what was happening to her because she thought it was normal and that they would be experiencing it too. Generally the children kept these family situations secret (ten of the 12 cases), and probably with good reason. One girl's mother, on finding her daughter being caressed by her stepfather, was angry and blamed the girl for encouraging him. In another case, where a girl had eventually told her mother, she soon felt guilty because the mother, apparently very upset, became strange and distant towards her. This girl's stepfather had also made advances to her elder and younger sisters, but they had told him to 'get off'. Her older sister tried to encourage her to do likewise but, as she did not, told an aunt. This lady informed the police with the result that the girl was taken into care. Her subsequent experiences with officialdom were described as 'embarrassing and frightening'. This was a lonely time for her, making her feel 'different' in every way:

No one ever wanted to help me mentally. The social worker was always 'very busy'. I could never sit down and really talk to her.

Only two women could state that they had come to terms with their feelings about past incestuous situations. Most felt some degree of resentment and guilt about what had happened, and even those who had married tended to be suspicious of men and their intentions:

I still hate my dad now. Sometimes I wish it was my dad that died instead of my mum. [Married with one child - has sex very rarely]

I'm disgusted at myself. I couldn't give a damn about him stepfather . [Single woman still very wary of all men]

I've kept all this bottled up for so long. The problem is that I can't speak openly. I feel dirty. I don't like

talking about sex. I'd like to talk to someone but I'm
scared they'll turn round and throw it in my face.
[Twenty year old, still unable to relate to men]

Where women had approached a professional for assistance
with sexual difficulties, attributed by them to their childhood sex experiences within the family, the advice tended to
be rather unfortunate, as in the following case:

I told him [third husband] before we got married. I had
to explain to him as I thought it wasn't a good idea to
get married...He was very good...he said that it wasn't my
fault, there was no reason to blame me...why didn't I go
to the doctor. I had been to my doctor in my previous
marriage and had explained that I had got a problem about
sex. He fixed an appointment with a psychiatrist and I
started. He didn't ask me and I didn't tell him that my
father had tried to have sex with me...and he said "You
are crying because your father hit you, and you deeply
love your father and you are crying because the relationship has broken down". So I couldn't talk to him any more,
and I didn't go back to him. I just can't bear the embarrassment of trying to tell anyone, I just can't do it...
it's terribly difficult talking to an outsider, but when
I've done it once it might be easier. I don't want this
marriage to fail and I know it will if this carries on, I
mean, no matter how much we love each other...it's awful.
I can't respond to my husband, I couldn't to the three of
them [husbands]. The only way in which I could be aroused,
I've had clitoral orgasm, but never a vaginal one. And
I've tried, and if there was no sex in marriage it would
be lovely. I can't respond, I just freeze...unless I have
a clitoral orgasm, I respond then...exactly the same as in
previous marriages...but it upsets me because the time between making love gets longer and longer. There is a ten-
sion now when we go to bed. That's why I know it's getting bad. He has been fairly active sexually...I feel he
should be getting a full marriage in a sexual way. I want
to respond but I just can't. We just lie next to each
other, but when he attempts to make love I can't respond.
I am just like a piece of wood...it's no fun for him...
unless I'm getting a climax...it will take hours...it's
awful.

7 Initial reactions and long term effects

DISCLOSURES

The questionnaire asked whether anyone was told about the in-
cident(s), and of the 94 respondents from the G.P. sample who
reported an experience 52 (55 per cent) said they had told no
one. Of the 50 students with experiences, 32 per cent had
told no one. This difference between the samples was statistically significant (χ^2 = 7.12, p<0.01). It may be that
students were more confiding because they were more likely
than the respondents from the G.P. sample to have been brought
up in homes where sexual matters were openly discussed.

In both our groups the child's mother was by far the most
likely confidante: 28 per cent of the students and 21 per
cent of those from the G.P. group who had an experience told
their mothers. Occasionally friends or other family members
were told and five students (ten per cent) and six from the
G.P. group (six per cent) had informed some person in
authority.

A majority of the questionnaire respondents who had told
someone (53 per cent from the student group, 62 per cent from
the G.P. sample) replied 'yes' in answer to the question whether or not their confidant had been helpful. This conflicted
with their descriptions of the reaction of the person told.
Only five (15 per cent) of the 34 students who told someone

and seven (17 per cent) of the 42 G.P. respondents who told someone felt that their confidant had been understanding or had bothered to explain to them what had happened. Most reported reactions were such as might be thought to be less than helpful to a distressed child, such as (in decreasing frequency) contacting the police, amusement, anger, respondent's story ignored, shock or surprise, desire for retribution, or respondent told to keep the incident secret.

At the subsequent interviews further details were obtained about the persons who had been told at the time, and their reactions. Out of the total of 138 encounters described at interview 67 (49 per cent) had been mentioned to someone - parent, girlfriend or otherwise - soon after the event. The reactions of the confidants are summarised in Table 7.1.

Table 7.1
Reactions of confidants when told of child/adult
sexual contact as recalled by adult interviewees*
Arranged in order of helpfulness

	No.	%
Comfort and understanding	16	24
Play it down	6	9
Amusement (peer confidants only)	12	18
Curiosity (peer confidants only)	5	7
Anger with perpetrator	17	25
Shock	14	21
Forbid the child going to that place again	8	12
Ignored or didn't care	6	9
Disbelief	4	6
Anger with child	5	7
Total incidents confided in someone	67	100

* N.B.   Individual reactions add up to more than the total number of incidents as some confidants reacted in more than one way.

61

The most common reactions on being told of an incident were
initial shock and anger towards the adult involved and sym-
pathy for the child. Most mothers tended to show concern for
the welfare of their daughters, whereas fathers tended to express more of a desire to seek retribution from the adult.
Thus, mothers were considered more helpful than fathers, whose
aggressively masculine response to a threat to one of his family could be counter-productive. In a previous study Gibbens
and Prince (1963) found that 25 per cent of the reactions of
parents of child sex victims aggravated the situation. In the
present study only a minority of the persons confided in by
the girls responded to the news in an appropriate manner.
Least helpful reactions were anger with the child, disbelief,
a dismissive attitude or an hysterical outburst. In such
cases respondents often became 'double victims' believing
themselves guilty for encouraging the sexual advances or blaming themselves for being the cause of parental upset. The
following was the experience of an eight year old who had been
molested for some time by a young employee of her father:

> My mother was hysterical for days. She cried and cried.
> My father was furious and went around shouting...I felt it
> was all my fault - that I was the cause of my mother's
> distress...My mother took me and asked me if he had ever
> touched me and what he'd done to me. At first I denied it
> and then I said he had. Then they put me into the spare
> bed until the doctor came. I was perfectly well and
> couldn't understand why the doctor was coming. Mother
> took me to bed and cried and cried and asked me to tell
> her how often it had happened and in the end I said a
> dozen times. Then the doctor came and (this went on over
> two or three days) and the doctor examined me on the din-
> ing table. He looked at me and confirmed that I was still
> a virgin. My parents heaved a sigh of relief then they
> told me never to talk to anyone about it, and it was never
> mentioned again...I think my parents handled it appall-
> ingly...They told me never ever to tell anyone again. If
> only they'd been able to talk about sex and explain that
> adult sex is not like that.

Although 71 of the 138 incidents described by the interviewees had been initially kept secret, a further 13 were
eventually discovered by a parent or sister. The reason most
frequently cited by the women for their initial secrecy was
that as children they had feared that their parents would
blame them (17 cases). Other similar reasons were feeling
ashamed (four cases), knowing it was wrong (four cases) or
thinking they would be taken away by police - an idea instig-
ated by some of the offenders (four cases). Some felt their
parents would be embarrassed (11 cases), others saw no need to

62

tell because they had not been upset in any way (ten cases).

Most of the interviewed women said they had not mentioned their early experiences to anyone since they had grown up. Of those who had done so, most had told a female friend or their male partner. In the opinion of these informants, women tended to empathise more than men. Police were informed at the time of the occurrence in 24 (17 per cent) of the incidents which were described at interview. This compares with six per cent in the study by Gagnon (1965) and ten per cent in the survey by Landis (1956). Those who had been interrogated by police had tended to find the questions humiliating, embarrassing or frightening. Police, social workers and G.P.s were often described as having failed to understand the child's feelings and to have made the situation worse. Some respondents suggested that it would have been less difficult for them if the officials involved had been female or if their parents had not been present during questioning. In spite of these comments, in 15 unnotified cases the women, looking back on the events, said they wished the police had been informed.

IMMEDIATE REACTIONS

The questionnaire respondents' comments in answer to the item: 'How did you feel about what happened at the time?' were classified by the researcher with the results illustrated in Figure 7.1. The majority of feelings at the time were said to have been negative, although 29 (31 per cent) of answers from the G.P. sample and 25 (50 per cent) from the students indicated that some of their feelings had been positive, such as enjoyment/excitement, curiosity or amusement. There is no apparent reason for the larger proportion of positive feelings expressed by the student group. (Only one student mentioned that the adult in question had been a boyfriend whereas four of the G.P. sample did so). However, the students, being younger and in a social environment possibly more conducive to frankness, might have felt less constrained than the G.P. sample to report only what they felt to be the more socially acceptable reactions. Feelings of shame and embarrassment at the time were more often reported by students, confusion was recalled more often in the replies from the G.P. sample.

The predominance of negative emotions immediately following the child/adult sexual contact agrees with previous research on the topic. Constantine (1981) reviewed 30 studies (12 on clinic populations, nine from legal sources and nine from elsewhere) which included some analysis of the impact on children of early sexual experiences with adults. All but one of

63

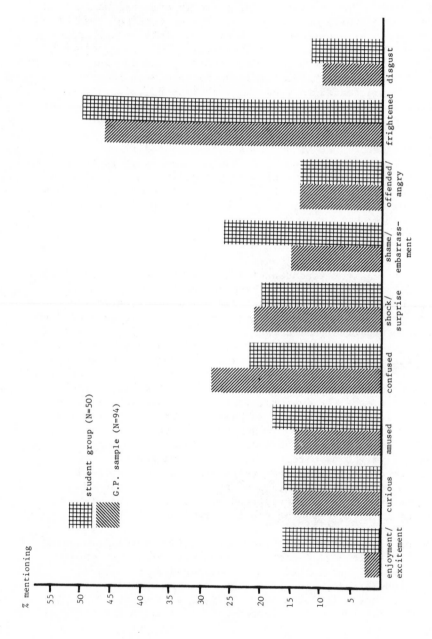

Figure 7.1 Reactions of children to sexual experiences with adults (questionnaire data)

the studies reported some negative outcomes. In the surveys
that are most comparable with our own, fear is the most commonly cited initial reaction on the part of the children
(Landis 1956, Gagnon 1965, Finkelhor 1979). Shock and curiosity are also frequently mentioned reactions.

Some of the detailed accounts of immediate childhood reactions obtained at interviews have already been described under
the separate categories of experience. For convenience, these
are summarised in Table 7.2. They serve to amplify and confirm the brief comments given on the questionnaires. On the
whole, the results bear out the findings of previous research.
Of our interviewed respondents, 55 per cent mentioned fear as
an initial response, compared with 58 per cent in the survey
by Finkelhor (1979). However, many more of our interviewees
(41 per cent as compared with eight per cent in Finkelhor's
study), acknowledged some degree of pleasure, excitement or
arousal. This cannot of course be equated with the experience
of consensual adult relationships. Many of those who said
they had been pleased at the attention or flattery which they
had received were at the same time confused and frightened.

LONG TERM EFFECTS

Previous research has come to various and conflicting conclusions regarding the effects of childhood sexual encounters
with adults. According to one view the very disparity in size
and social sophistication between children and adults render
such encounters inherently traumatic (Oremland and Oremland
1977). Card (1975), whilst accepting that there are risks of
mental or physical harm where very young girls are concerned,
states that even here any ill effects are generally short term.
Kinsey et al. (1953, p.121), go further and state, 'it is difficult to understand why a child, except for its cultural con-
ditioning, should be disturbed at having its genitalia touched,
or disturbed at seeing the genitalia of other persons, or disturbed at even more specific sexual contacts'. Lending some
support to the latter view is a review of studies by Powell
and Chalkley (1981) which conclude that adult/child sexual
contacts have no damaging effects on children, and articles by
Brongersma (1977 and 1980), who goes further, claiming that
children can have pleasant memories of sexual encounters with
adults and that some adult victims would wish their own children to have similar experiences. Despite such assertions, it
seems wise to bear in mind the warning of Steele and Alexander
(1981, p.233), namely, that 'much pain and turmoil might exist
beneath an outwardly normal or seemingly well adjusted appearance'. Indeed, much previous research has found the outcomes

Table 7.2

Immediate childhood reactions to sexual encounters with adults as remembered by adult interviewees

Percentage of incidents in which various reactions were noted

Type of Reaction	Verbal suggestion		Obscene 'phone call		Exhibitionism (includes six more serious repeated incidents)		Sexual kiss		Non-genital fondling		Genital fondling		Attempted intercourse		Intercourse		All incidents	% of 78 interviewees mentioning
	No.	%	No.	%	No.	%	No.	%	No.	%	No.	%	No.	%	No.	%	No.	No.
Pain	-	-	-	-	-	-	-	-	3	18	1	5	2	17	9	75	15	19
Fear	15	38	4	80	9	22	3	18	5	29	9	43	7	58	1	8	43	55
Blocked/can't remember	-	-	-	-	-	-	-	-	2	12	3	14	1	8	1	8	7	9
Indifference	2	15	2	40	6	15	1	6	-	-	2	10	1	8	1	8	15	19
Pleasure/arousal	5	38	-	-	1	2	6	35	3	18	7	33	5	42	5	42	32	41
Repulsion	3	23	-	-	1	2	6	35	3	18	4	19	1	8	4	33	22	28
Amusement	2	15	-	-	26	63	-	-	1	6	-	-	-	-	-	-	29	37
Shock/confusion	3	23	4	80	20	49	10	59	9	53	7	33	3	25	1	8	57	73
Attempt to get away	2	15	-	-	18	44	4	24	4	24	4	19	1	8	1	8	34	44
Thought it was wrong	4	30	-	-	2	5	3	18	3	18	3	14	1	8	-	-	16	21
Total no. of incidents (=100%)	13		5		41		17		17		21		12		12		138	

N.B. Respondents frequently mentioned more than one reaction to an incident: responses, therefore, total more than incidents.

66

of childhood sexual encounters to be largely negative (Constantine 1981, Mrazek and Mrazek 1981). This is particularly true where selected samples such as prostitutes (James and Meyerding 1978, Silbert and Pines 1981) and psychiatric clients (Bender and Blau 1937, Weiner 1962, Meiselman 1978) are concerned, but of course causal relationships cannot be substantiated by selective retrospective studies.

Our own findings, in conformity with the conflicting results of previous surveys, were that reported long term effects were extremely variable, often absent altogether, but sometimes seriously and possibly permanently damaging. From the item on the questionnaire which asked those who had had a relevant experience to say how long they had been affected, it emerged that 50 (53 per cent) of the respondents from the G.P. sample who had had some experience, and 26 (52 per cent) from the student sample, described no negative effects or none which lasted more than a few weeks. Nevertheless, five (ten per cent) of the student and 12 (13 per cent) of the G.P. respondents mentioned effects lasting a year or more, and a significant minority - 11 (22 per cent) of student victims and 13 (14 per cent) of the G.P. victims - considered themselves to be still affected by their experiences.

On the item concerning their present feelings, the majority of questionnaire respondents - 34 (68 per cent) from the student group and 70 (74 per cent) from the G.P. sample - mentioned indifference as at least one of their current sentiments. Interestingly, although some respondents remembered their reaction at the time in relatively positive terms, none did so on looking back on their experience with adult eyes. The closest to a positive sentiment was pity for the adult concerned. In the student group 26 per cent had remembered experiencing shame or embarrassment at the time of the incident, but none of these expressed shame or guilt in retrospect. In the G.P. sample, however, 12 per cent reported still feeling guilt or shame, much the same as at the time it happened. Guilt has been referred to by other researchers as a more frequent reaction than was the case in the present study (Constantine 1981, Finkelhor 1979). Possibly the recent British media coverage of sexually abused women, highlighting their status as victims, has served to reduce guilt. In the G.P. sample, the proportion who felt angry at the time of the sexual contact was similar to that who felt angry about it on looking back. In the student group more expressed anger in retrospect than had done so at the time of the incident. The findings are illustrated in Figure 7.2.

Some of the detailed descriptions of continuing, long term

% mentioning

Figure 7.2 Present feelings about their past childhood sexual experiences with adults reported by questionnaire respondents

effects attributed to early sexual experiences, which were obtained during the follow up interviews, have already been cited under the headings of the different types of sexual experience. An analysis of the present feelings of all the interviewed women, on looking back at what happened to them, is shown in Table 7.3. Again, this served to amplify the briefer comments returned on the questionnaires.

The majority of interviewed women continued to express predominantly negative feelings. The more serious long term disturbances attributed to early trauma (such as sexual or emotional difficulties, mistrust of all men, guilt and continued hatred or resentment of the adult involved) tended to be associated with the more serious forms of abuse (genital fondling, attempted intercourse and full intercourse). This agrees with the study by Landis (1956) which also showed increased frequency of reported emotional damage with greater sexual involvement. In the present study, where there had been a large disparity in age (30+ years) between the child and the adult, this tended to be associated with continuing emotional or sexual difficulties. A small age difference (five to ten years) was associated with regret for what had happened and, markedly, with confusion over sexual norms between adults and children.

Feelings of mere indifference to what had happened were commoner if it was a stranger who had made the sexual approach. Landis (1956) also found a lower rate of reported emotional damage where the offender was a stranger. In contrast, sexual experience with family friends tended to leave the women with an attitude of wariness towards, or avoidance of, men in general. Retrospectively, a certain amount of pity was also felt for these friends and neighbours. Pity and amusement were the most often expressed sentiments towards the authority figures (such as vicars) who had made sexual advances. Looking back, some women were amused by the tentative sexual attempts of older boyfriends, but more were left wondering about sexual mores. Sexual contact with fathers left the women even more confused. Experiences with stepfathers or uncles tended to leave them with bitter feelings such as anger, hatred and resentment. Current emotional and/or sexual difficulties tended to be attributed particularly to experiences with fathers and brothers and sometimes to experiences with strangers if they had been violent.

In the light of their present knowledge, many women believed that there was nothing they could have done to avoid the sexual contact which they had suffered. Eighteen of the interviewed women who had such experiences in childhood (23 per cent) felt that girls should be taught by parents or teachers

Table 7.3
Long term effects of child/adult sexual encounters (interview data)

| Type of effect | Percentage of incidents from which various effects were noted | | | | | | | | | | | | | | | | | | All incidents | % of 78 interviewees mentioning |
| | Verbal suggestion | | Obscene 'phone call | | Exhibitionism (includes six more serious repeated incidents) | | Sexual kiss | | Non-genital fondling | | Genital fondling | | Attempted intercourse | | Intercourse | | | |
	No.	%	No.	%	No.	%	No.	%	No.	%	No.	%	No.	%	No.	%	No.	
Indifference, worked through	5	38	4	80	13	32	9	53	3	18	5	24	3	25	3	25	45	58
Regret	–	–	–	–	8	20	6	35	6	35	5	24	2	17	5	42	32	41
Hatred/resentment towards adult	1	8	–	–	4	10	1	6	5	29	5	24	7	58	5	42	28	36
Wary of all men	5	38	–	–	8	20	1	6	9	53	14	67	5	42	–	–	41	53
Confused re. sexual norms	3	23	–	–	6	15	4	24	7	41	1	5	–	–	4	33	25	32
Emotional/sexual dysfunction	–	–	–	–	1	2	–	–	3	18	6	29	1	8	6	50	17	22
Anxiety for other children	3	23	–	–	8	20	–	–	1	6	6	29	1	8	1	8	20	26
Guilt/disgust	2	16	–	–	2	4	1	6	5	29	5	24	5	42	9	75	38	49
Anger	1	8	4	80	20	49	1	6	11	65	10	48	4	33	3	25	54	69
Pity/amusement	2	16	–	–	29	71	10	59	7	41	4	19	3	25	–	–	55	71
Total no. of incidents (=100%)	13		5		41		17		17		21		12		12		138	

N.B. Respondents frequently mentioned several feelings: percentages do not, therefore, total 100.

how to cope with sexually provocative males - a view shared by
some NSPCC officials. Twelve (15 per cent) felt that little
could be done as the behaviour was a normal feature of male
sexuality. In spite of the probable difficulties in voicing
such admissions, there were 14 incidents (ten per cent) in
which the women concerned felt that they could have avoided
the situation. Two women believed that they had been entirely
to blame for their sexual encounters and three women expressed
regret for the abrupt ending of a relationship from which they
had been deriving some satisfaction. Virkunnen (1975, 1981)
has referred to such incidents as 'victim precipitated' and to
the children involved as 'participating victims'. They would
also fall into the 'true consent' category of Lafon et al.
(1961), where the child participates in the act. Burton (1968)
who interviewed victims whilst they were still children suggests that there is usually a degree of child participation,
and that little trauma follows unless the child was already
disturbed, but neither of these contentions fits the retrospective descriptions of the majority of the women interviewed
in this study.

8 Comparisons between women with and without a history of sexual abuse as children

DIFFERENCES WHEN CHILDREN

The data from this study provided some information on features that distinguished the 'abused' women from those who said they had not been 'abused'. The total numbers of women available for comparison were as indicated in Figure 4.1, p.18, but of course on some items the information was not available for every questionnaire or interview respondent.

It has been suggested by previous investigators that sexual abuse of female children is more prevalent amongst the lower socio-economic classes (BASPCAN 1981, Finkelhor 1979, Weinberg 1955). This was not found to be so in the present study. The most relevant information on the topic came from the question-naires returned from the G.P. sample, in which the whole range of social classes was well represented. Judged by the repor-ted occupations of their fathers during their childhood, and the present occupation of the main wage earner in the home, there was no significant difference between the 'abused' and 'non-abused' women in either socio-economic class of origin or present socio-economic class. The figures are displayed in Table 8.1.

There was some suggestion, from information provided by the interviewed women, that those with a history of abuse were less likely to have received further education beyond standard

Table 8.1

Socio-economic class of origin and present
socio-economic class of questionnaire respondents from G.P. sample

| | 'Abused' women | | | | 'Non-abused' | | | |
| | Original socio-economic class | | Present socio-economic class | | Original socio-economic class | | Present socio-economic class | |
Occupation	No.	%	No.	%	No.	%	No.	%
Manual	45	48	29	31	67	52	50	39
Non-manual	40	43	56	60	51	39	70	54
Students, unem-ployed, services	9	9	9	9	11	9	9	7
Total	94	100	94	100	129	100	129	100

schooling. Ignoring those from the student group (who had all, by definition, gone on to higher education), among the 'abused' women who gave the necessary information 37 per cent (19 out of 51), compared with 65 per cent (15 out of 23) of 'non-abused' women had had further education (χ^2 = 4.99, p<0.03). If further education reflects higher intelligence or social sophistication, then these qualities among the 'non-abused' women might possible have rendered them less vulnerable to molestation, or better equipped to avoid it.

Lukianowicz (1972) found that 70 per cent of the incestuous fathers in his study were unemployed at a time of high employ-ment. In our study two of the three women who said that their fathers were unemployed during all or most of their childhood had been sexually abused by them. Most of our respondents had been brought up in cities, and most of the incidents reported had taken place in cities. No consistent correlation between living in the country and experience of abuse could be detected.

The 109 interviewed women were questioned about their family upbringing, and 27 per cent of the 'abused' group (12 of 77, one gave no information) compared with only 13 per cent (four of 31) of the 'non-abused' said they had been brought up other than by both natural parents. A difference of this kind, showing that anomalous family situations were more prevalent among the 'abused', is in line with the previous work of De Francis (1969), Finkelhor (1979) and - in regard to 'collabor-ative' children - of Landis (1956).

Tormes (1968), in investigating social services records of abused children in America, found that it was oldest daughters who were the ones most vulnerable to sexual approaches from their fathers, but this trend was not apparent, either in Finkelhor's more extensive work (1979) or in the present study.

It has been suggested that vulnerability to sexual abuse may be passed on from mother to daughter, since women who have themselves been badly affected may become inadequate mothers and appear to collude with male abusers (Goodwin 1982, Renvoize 1982). We had no means of investigating this, since the women were unlikely to be aware of their mother's sexual history. Nevertheless, one woman who described herself as having been persecuted by a fondling and masturbating older brother (mostly between the ages of ten and 13) said:

> My mother knew about it and what I didn't know at the time was that she had had an incestuous relationship with her father between the ages of seven and 19. Mother knew all about what was going on...She tried to get my father to do

74

something about it. She said that she felt all the same
feelings for me that she had felt but she couldn't do anything to help me, she said that there was nothing she
could do to get out of her room to protect me. It was awful for her...she was totally helpless. In fact she did
try to get my father to do something but he was hopeless.
She went to the doctor and he told her that it would be
all right and that he would grow out of it when he got a
girlfriend. It seems incredible now, that complete lack
of concern for the girl involved and the horrors that I
was going through. It was completely orientated to him
growing out of it...it was absolutely amazing that there
was no concern about me at all. My mother felt that there
was no recourse to anyone.

Most of the interviewed women (74 per cent) described their
upbringing as having been fairly strict, with rules for permitted times for coming home and permitted places to go and
punishments for disobedience. The 'abused' and 'non-abused'
were no different in this respect.

Finkelhor (1979) and Newman (1983) found a positive relationship between marital conflict and disruption in the parental home and incidence of child sexual abuse. This did not
emerge in the present study. Parental divorce and memories of
quarrels between parents were similar among both the 'abused'
and 'non-abused' women. Slightly more of the 'abused' than of
the 'non-abused' interviewees reported having been estranged
from, or rejected by, parents, or having been closer to their
grandparents than to their parents (19 of 78, 24 per cent,
against six of 31, 19 per cent), but the difference was
minimal.

In response to the questionnaire item asking about whether
their childhood had been happy, a much larger proportion of
the 'abused' respondents reported unhappiness, the difference
being particularly marked in those from the larger G.P. sample
(see Table 8.2). For the total of questionnaire respondents,
the difference between the 'abused' and 'non-abused' respondents in the proportion of unhappy childhoods was statistically very significant (χ^2 = 18.3, p<0.01). Of course it is
impossible to know whether the unhappiness preceded the sexual
abuse, was a consequence of it, or was a retrospective eval-
uation influenced by a later acquired cultural abhorrence of
paedophilia. It is difficult to understand why unhappiness
was reported so much more frequently than other indications of
disturbed home circumstances, such as parental conflict or
over-strict discipline.

Table 8.2
Level of happiness in childhood (questionnaire data)

| | G.P. sample | | | | Student group | | | |
| | 'Abused' women | | 'Non-abused' | | 'Abused' women | | 'Non-abused' | |
	No.	%	No.	%	No.	%	No.	%
Happy	62	67	117	91	37	76	36	88
Not happy	31	33	12	9	12	24	5	12
Total	93*	100	129	100	49*	100	41*	100

* One respondent in each of these groups gave no information.

Finkelhor (1979) emphasises the role of the mother in transmitting sound sex information to daughters. The questionnaire asked about the main sources of sexual information in childhood. Table 8.3 sets out the responses. The student group, more often than the G.P. sample, mentioned information from mother rather than from school lessons, but in neither sample was there any noticeable difference between the 'abused' and the 'non-abused' in their major sources of information.

In the British magazine survey it was found that 'in the abused group, mothers had been likely to be stricter in dealing with their children's sexual upbringing, to be more punitive about children's curiosity concerning sex generally' (Newman 1983, p.39). In so far as there was any such trend in this study it was in the opposite direction. Among the interviewed women with a history of abuse 38 per cent (30 of 78) said their parents had been frank and open in dealing with sexual matters. Among the 'non-abused' only 23 per cent (seven of 31) said this. Among the 'non-abused' women 58 per cent (18 of 31) said that in their parental homes sex was a taboo subject. Among the 'abused' women a smaller proportion, 46 per cent (36 of 78) made that comment. It could be that children brought up in a sexually open environment are less embarrassed and readier to recall their sexual incidents with adults.

Family nudity is a controversial subject which might be relevant. Some believe that it is useful and fosters positive gender identity (Oremland and Oremland 1977) whilst others

Table 8.3

Questionnaire respondents' major sources of sexual knowledge in childhood*

| | G.P. sample | | | | Student group | | | |
| | 'Abused' women | | 'Non-abused' | | 'Abused' women | | 'Non-abused' | |
Source	number mentioning (N=94)	%	number mentioning (N=129)	%	number mentioning (N=50)	%	number mentioning (N=42)	%
None	6	6	6	5	3	6	3	7
Boyfriend	15	16	14	11	4	8	–	–
Self-discovery	16	17	23	18	9	18	2	5
Female peers	32	24	34	26	15	30	17	40
Mother	32	34	38	29	25	50	24	57
Father	1	1	3	2	5	10	1	2
School lessons	38	40	57	44	12	24	16	38
Older brother	1	1	2	2	3	6	1	2
Book/TV	23	24	30	23	16	32	13	31
Dirty jokes	3	3	4	3	–	–	3	7

* N.B. Some respondents mentioned more than one source. Percentages do not, therefore, total 100.

maintain that excessive nudity leads to anxiety and confusion in the minds of younger children (Steele and Alexander 1981). Results from the present study would appear to indicate that, as with a frank attitude to sex, a liberal attitude to nudity affords no protection from sexual abuse. Fourteen of the 109 interviewees had seen their father or elder brother(s) naked; 12 of these had suffered childhood sexual abuse; four interviewees had seen a younger brother naked and three of these had suffered childhood sexual abuse. Both of the two interviewees who had witnessed their parents' love-making had suffered childhood sexual abuse. In the work of Kinsey et al. (1953) it was found that 45 per cent of females had observed adult male genitalia by age 15 and even at age seven, 20 per cent had done so. The much lower incidence in the present study may reflect differing levels of modesty in Britain and the USA.

It could be that early sexual experience of any kind contributes to the likelihood of experiencing sexual abuse. Indeed, when interviewees were quizzed about their sexual activity with other children, it was found that 51 per cent (16 of 31) among the 'non-abused', compared to only 27 per cent (21 of 78) of those approached sexually by adults, had never indulged in peer group sex games (χ^2 = 6.0, p<0.02). The 'abused' women were not only more likely to have engaged in mutual childhood sexual exploration, but also to have continued to do so for longer. Twenty-two per cent (17 of 78) were still involved in such activity after the age of ten, compared to only three per cent (one of 31) of the 'non-abused' interviewees.

Much has been said about telling children not to accept sweets or lifts from strangers (with or without an explanation), and it may be that most parents give their offspring such advice, but only a minority of our interviewed women could remember ever being warned. Ten per cent (three) of the 'non-abused' and (prior to the encounter with an adult) 33 per cent (26) of the 'abused' recalled such warnings. This difference between the 'abused' and 'non-abused' was statistically significant (χ^2 = 6.4, p<0.02). It may be that girls perceived to be more vulnerable on account of their more forward behaviour with adults were more likely to provoke parental warnings. Alternatively, it could be that girls who subsequently had untoward sexual experiences with adults would be forcibly reminded of warnings which others would have forgotten.

DIFFERENCES AS ADULTS

The interviewed women who defined their social life as solitary - that is having no hobbies, or at least none outside the
home - were marginally fewer among the 'abused' than the 'non-
abused' (36 of 78 against 16 of 31). However, all of the
spare time of two of the 'abused' women was taken up with feminist groups, and both of them had reassessed their childhood
experiences in terms of feminist ideas. Thus one woman who
recalled a full sexual relationship with a man from the age of
14, referred to her own curiosity about how she had let
herself be 'used' as 'feminine masochism'.

The interviewed women were asked about the age when they
first engaged in coitus (two childhood experiences with adults
excluded). The results are shown in Table 8.4.

Table 8.4
Age at first coitus (interview data)

Age	'Abused' women		'Non-abused'	
	No.	%	No.	%
<16	17	22	1	3
16-18	20	26	9	29
18+	35	45	21	68
Never	6	8	-	-
Total	78	100	31	100

A much higher proportion of the 'abused' than the 'non-
abused' women reported an early start to peer group coitus.
It does not follow that this led to promiscuity, although such
a sequel of child sex abuse (particularly incest) has been
noted by some researchers (Steele and Alexander 1981, Mrazek
and Mrazek 1981, Meiselman 1978). The 'abused' women were
less likely to retain their virginity until they were engaged
or married. A few among both the 'abused' and 'non-abused'
women felt that their first coitus had been forced upon them
(see Table 8.5).

Table 8.5

Reasons given by interviewees for first coitus

	'Abused' women		'Non-abused'	
	No.	%	No.	%
Unwilling i.e. rape or forced intercourse	8	11	2	7
Willing i.e. planned, love or curiosity	49	68	17	56
Engaged or married	15	21	11	36
Total	72	100	30*	100

* One woman gave no reason.

Some women who have been sexually abused as children continue to be victims in adult life (Goodwin and Owen 1982). The idea that subsequent sexual behaviour can be related to early sexual experiences is discussed by Nelson (1982) who argues that if a woman learnt, as a child, that she was only good for sex, her consequent self disgust and low self esteem may render her open to sexual abuse as an adult. Interviewees in the present study were questioned on their experiences (if any) of sexual harassment after the age of 16. No significant differences were found between the 'abused' and the 'non-abused' in the proportions who reported some harassment (49 of 78 against 21 of 31), although a slightly greater proportion of the 'abused' had experienced rape or attempted rape (see Table 8.6).

It could be argued that the women who have been sexually abused as children are thereby sensitised to later harassment and perhaps readier to define sexual incidents in negative terms. One woman, who claimed to have been 'raped' on three separate occasions by the same man, admitted that she did not consider herself raped at the time, but only since she developed an awareness of the inferior position of women in society. Despite her assertive reassessment of the facts, she still appeared confused over her own role in the 'rape'. As a child of ten to 13 she had been subjected to fondling by a brother and exhibitionism by her father.

Table 8.6

Unsolicited adult sexual contact (interview data)

Type of contact	'Abused' women (N=78)		'Non-abused' (N=31)	
	No.	% of women mentioning	No.	% of women mentioning
Exhibitionist	19	24	9	29
Obscene telephone calls	23	29	9	29
Harassment e.g. bottom pinching	47	60	15	48
Rape and attempted rape	14	18	4	13
Total no. of incidents	103	-	37	-

N.B. Percentages do not total 100 as one interviewee could mention more than one type of incident.

81

I've been raped, I was 16. It was the same person three
times. I think I just couldn't believe it had happened
and I really didn't want it and being in that position you
have got to have it and the second time I remember that I
was having a period and the tampax went right up me and I
just tried to pretend it hadn't happened. It was horrible,
it was only recently that I would say that I had been
raped I really would have changed my image of rape. I
think he would have been in his thirties. It happened
when we were in the castle grounds in [X] and he started
kissing me and it wasn't acknowledged as a rape by him or
me. The second time he took me to a relative's house and
we went upstairs to bed and then he wouldn't stop and the
third time it was in the back of a garage and it was
standing up. I couldn't believe that it was happening...
I think I compromised and said that something bad had happened. Afterwards I used to try to avoid him and I was
afraid for my reputation. I thought he could use it
against me. It's very difficult to understand, it's a
sort of denial...and the thing was that I couldn't accept
that it didn't stop when I wanted it...I just couldn't believe that it would happen again and I couldn't accept
that I had been raped. It is very much later that I saw
those things as rapes.

Q. What time of day was it?

A. Twice in the night and once during the day. The first one
was during the day.

Q. Did you feel responsible for that one?

A. Yes, because...no...I don't think so, I thought the rules
were that you go as far as you want but basically one can
stop, and I thought the rules weren't being obeyed and
didn't go to the police...no I don't feel responsible for
it. I felt pretty furious about it and that I should have
learned...being feminine and that and that there was a
kind of inevitability about it...I saw men in a particular
way and I feel about it that it was part of a whole way of
being that has damaged me...making me helpless even when
being attacked.

Other women felt that the cutoff point for childhood at age
16 was arbitrary and that their own sexual experiences with
older men, when they were still too young to cope emotionally,
should have been included. For example, one respondent among
the 'non-abused' women, said that, as a 16 year old girl, when
she was acting as an au pair in Paris, she was raped by her
employer while his wife was in hospital having a baby. She
eventually requested a transfer from the family, but felt

unable to explain her reasons.

Women with no history of child sexual abuse seemed to re-
cover from the effects of adult harassment more rapidly and
easily. The women who had been 'abused' in the past appeared
to be more aware of their legal rights when harassed in adult
life; four contacted the police about it, whereas none did so
among the 'non-abused' group.

Aversion to sex (Greenland 1958), sexual dysfunctions and
character disorders (Lukianowicz 1972), unsatisfactory sexual
relationships (Rosenfeld et al. 1977), sexual dysfunction
(Meiselman 1978) and difficulties in establishing close relationships (Steele and Alexander 1981) have all been claimed
as possible sequelae of child sexual abuse. When the interviewed women in this study were asked about their current attitudes to sex significantly more of the 'abused' women
expressed negative feelings (23 of 78 against three of 31,
$\chi^2 = 4.8$, $p<0.05$).

Interviewees were also questioned on the frequency of intercourse and their relationships with their male partner (if
any). Table 8.7 shows the previously 'abused' women were less
likely than the 'non-abused' to be participating in regular
sexual activity. Most notably nine per cent (seven) of them
had never enjoyed an adult to adult sexual relationship and
another 24 per cent (19) had had no sexual intercourse in the
previous month.

Table 8.8 shows that the 'abused' women also tended to respond less positively when asked about their emotional relationship with their current male partner, and also that a far
larger percentage of them were without a male partner
($\chi^2 = 6.11$, $p<0.02$). The promiscuity highlighted by certain
authors (Lukianowicz 1972, Mrazek and Mrazek 1981) was not
found in this study. Only one woman stated that she was currently involved with numerous sexual partners, and she was
without a history of child sexual abuse.

These findings support the contentions of authorities who
suggest that early sexual experiences with adults are sometimes followed by adverse features in adult emotional and sexual function. The relationship need not be causal, however,
since there are undoubtedly other factors, such as personality,
family upbringing and life experiences, which may be antecedent causes of both sexual maladjustment and vulnerability to
childhood molestation. Moreover, it must be bourne in mind
that retrospective enquiries such as this are dependent upon
self report. Some individuals may have a bias to reporting

Table 8.7
Frequency of intercourse reported by interviewed women*

Frequency	'Abused' women		'Non-abused'	
	No.	%	No.	%
Never	7	9	1	3
Not in the last month	19	24	4	13
At least once in the last month	23	29	5	16
At least once a week	28	36	20	65
Pregnant	1	1	1	3
Total	78	100	31	100

* Willing intercourse only. Child/adult intercourse
and adult rape excluded.

Table 8.8
Emotional relationship with male partner (interview data)

Relationship	'Abused' women		'Non-abused'	
	No.	%	No.	%
Good or adequate relationship	48	62	24	77
Bad relationship or about to split	8	10	4	13
No male partner	22	28	2	7
Many male partners	-	-	1	3
Total	78	100	31	100

all sexual situations in an unfavourable light. There is at
least a possibility that this could lead to an apparent association between childhood abuse, later sexual harassment and
adult sexual problems, which is more a reflection of individual
attitudes than of objective reality.

In order to assess the effect of a history of child sex abuse on adult women's opinions of how these matters should be
dealt with, all the interviewed women were invited to put forward their own ideas. Reactions were very varied. They are
summarised in Table 8.9.

Women with a history of abuse were more often punitive,
wanting perpetrators killed, castrated or imprisoned. Those
without abusive histories were more likely to believe that men
who are sexually aroused by children are in need of psychiatric treatment. Interestingly, of the 'abused' women four
felt that nothing needed to be done since adult sexual interest in children is natural. The reasoning behind both this
reaction and the more punitive ones could be similar. Women
who have been abused by men well known to them as children,
and accepted as normal in every other way, may conclude that
sexual interest in children is normal and so can only be pre-
vented by physical constraint. Psychiatric treatment would
have no value in their eyes if they do not consider the
perpetrators to be mentally disturbed in any way.

Table 8.9

Opinions of interviewed women on how to deal with
child sexual abuse

Action considered appropriate	'Abused' women		'Non-abused'	
	No.	%	No.	%
Imprisonment of perpetrator	18	23	5	16
Fine perpetrator	–	–	1	3
Social Services	12	16	4	13
Separate adult and child	8	10	1	3
Psychiatric treatment for offender	17	22	15	48
Kill or castrate offender	15	20	2	7
Nothing – considered natural	4	5	–	–
Don't know	3	4	3	10
Total	78	100	31	100

9 Conclusions

LIMITATIONS OF THE PRESENT STUDY

The methodological difficulties intrinsic to a retrospective
enquiry into a sensitive topic can never be fully overcome.
Bias introduced through inadequate sampling is a particular
danger. During preliminary work an approach was made to a
student anti-sexism group (not included in the study) and it
was discovered that every female member claimed to have experienced sexual molestation from an adult during her childhood. It may be that women (especially intellectual women)
who have undergone such experiences are made more aware of the
social inequality of the sexes and are thus drawn to such
groups. Alternatively, it could be that women who are concerned about the vulnerability of the female sex, and are attempting to alter society by joining such groups, are more
ready to recall their early sexual experiences with adults, or
to reinterpret early experiences with adults in sexual terms.
In either case, such selective samples introduce a probability
of bias. The decision to use a random sample taken from a
G.P. register was probably successful in limiting this source
of bias, but of course could do nothing about the bias that
may have been introduced by the substantial proportion of nonrespondents. However, those who responded only after a further reminder did not appear to differ from the initial respondents in their replies, which suggests that this source of
bias may be less than might otherwise be expected.

Nevertheless, it seems likely that the women who felt most strongly about their childhood experiences, or who were still upset by them, were over-represented among those who volunteered for interview. It was noticeable that, in comparison with the total of questionnaire respondents, the interviewed women more often mentioned adverse long term reactions such as guilt/disgust and less often reported indifference (see Table 7.3, p.70).

Other difficulties include the inevitable forgetting of long past or more trivial events, the possible selectivity in recalling or reporting of more significant or more unpleasant experiences, and the likelihood of early experiences being re-interpreted in the light of attitudes developed in adulthood and influenced by other peoples' opinions. These were all factors that could not be eliminated, so one has to be aware of their possible effects when interpreting the results. Nevertheless, having completed and analysed so many interviews with individuals of varying opinions and social backgrounds, we may have got closer to reality than more restricted surveys of special groups. The tentative conclusions we have drawn may provide some guidelines for future research.

This study has concurred with previous work in finding that some women attribute long term emotional and/or sexual difficulties to childhood sexual experience with adults. Although some of the interviewees wished to put their unpleasant memories to the back of their minds after assisting with the research, others were distressed and felt the need for some form of therapy. They were provided with a list of helpful organisations, both local and in London, and a few were referred directly for professional assistance. In any further research on this topic the uncovering of similar needs should be anticipated.

TENTATIVE CONCLUSIONS

This study has shown evidence of a high incidence of child/adult sexual contacts. Types of experience differ widely - many are relatively trivial and some quite serious. Very few are reported to the authorities. Indeed, children often tell no one at all of such experiences.

It is impossible to isolate factors which will predict whether or not a child will have such experiences. Nevertheless some factors, notably an unhappy childhood, were found to be statistically more frequent among those women who recalled sexual contacts with adults when they were children. Other

factors discovered at interviews to be more characteristic of
the 'abused' than the 'non-abused' women included indulgence
in sex games in childhood, recollections of being warned by
parents against unknown adults, having no further education
beyond ordinary schooling, engaging in coitus under 18, having
a negative attitude to sex and having no current male partner.
The 'abused' women were particularly conscious of female vulnerability and sensitive to sexual harassment. Whilst this
might be a consequence of their early experiences it might
equally well be a cause of their remembering such experiences
more readily than other women. It is possible, also, that women with a 'feminist' attitude were over-represented among
those who responded to the questionnaire and agreed to be interviewed. Students who claimed to have had long term effects
from their early experiences with older men were more vocifer-
ous in their accounts than similarly affected women from the
G.P. sample.

In their current attitudes to sex the interviewed women who
recalled early 'abuse', compared with the 'non-abused' interviewees, appeared to run to two extremes, either becoming sexually active at an unusually early age or tending to withdraw
from adult sex. Thus, a higher proportion of 'abused' than
'non-abused' women reported having had their first coitus with
an age peer when they were under 16. On the other hand, a
higher proportion expressed negative feelings about adult sex
and some (nine per cent) had never willingly experienced adult
intercourse at all. Beliefs about how to deal with child sexual abuse were also more extreme among women who had themselves been 'abused'. Many felt that perpetrators should be
killed, castrated or imprisoned. Far fewer of the 'non-abused'
women expressed these punitive views. The need to separate
known offenders from the child with whom they had been involved
was a first consideration in the minds of women who had had
such experiences. Often these women expressed concern over
the vulnerability of their own children. In contrast, women
who had had no experience of adult/child sexual contact were
more likely to believe that psychiatric treatment was all that
was necessary in order to rehabilitate the offender.

Most researchers, especially those seeking in-depth data,
have concentrated on incest and often on those victims known
by various agencies to have been upset in some way by their
experiences. The present study places incest in the much
wider context of child sexual abuse. Only five of the 138 experiences recounted by interviewees were perpetrated by a bio-
logical father, and in only one of these cases did penetration
occur, making the incident incest in a legal sense. Nevertheless, though they rarely amount to incest, sexual experiences

in childhood often consist of more than casual encounters with a 'flasher' or involvement in group sex games with older children. Whilst one can reasonably assume that sexual violence or paternal incest are traumatic for the child, with potentially far reaching effects, it is not necessarily correct to regard seemingly less serious incidents as inconsequential. Children react very differently according to individual personality and background. Stable families with loving relationships and a healthy open attitude towards sexuality probably afford some protection, but ultimately it is the individual child's assessment of any sexual contact with an adult and her reaction to it (whether extreme or not) which determines whether or not the event will affect her adversely.

The majority of incidents were kept secret by the children involved, mostly from fear of being blamed. Those who did confide in a parent, and those whose experiences were notified to authorities, were often met by reactions which seemed to them to make matters worse or added to anxiety and guilt. The following example stands for many similar cases:

> At some time after this happened my parents found out and there was an awful fuss. I completely "forgot" about i.e. repressed the whole incident (or rather, series of incidents). Later, when I began to have sexual experiences as a teenager I remembered everything. How it has affected my sex life now I can't tell. My main feeling about it all was that it was somehow my fault that my mother was so upset. I grew up in a home where sex was dirty and unmentionable and my parents' response reinforced this view. I have tried hard since to clear these Victorian views out of my mind. I think I've not been entirely successful.

When sexual abuse of a young girl is disclosed the reactions of the adults around her are often problematic and liable to aggravate her distress. Intuitive recognition of the possibility of such unfavourable reactions is probably in large part responsible for children's secrecy about these matters. Parents who have made it known that they are available to be consulted in any crisis and who are non-condemnatory in sexual matters will more likely be told at once if their child has been distressed by a sexual encounter. Their reactions can help or hinder her subsequent adjustment to it.

RECOMMENDATIONS FOR FURTHER RESEARCH

The present enquiry was intended as no more than an exploratory study of a difficult topic about which reliable information is scarce. Although inevitably somewhat superficial, it has yielded data to supplement the findings of similar American surveys. The results highlight, more than anything, the need for further and more comprehensive investigation.

A long term prospective study of a cohort of normal children would be an ideal design. This type of research has been done in the field of male delinquency (West 1982). The high incidence of reported sexual experiences in childhood makes it feasible to envisage a similar research centred on sexual molestation and its sequelae among a normal population. This would provide a built-in group of unmolested children with which to compare, both in background and in outcome, the progress of the molested children. This could not fail to yield a more accurate assessment of the significance of the experiences of childhood sexual contacts with adults, as well as providing data on any intervening factors (such as untoward reactions following disclosure) which might have an influence upon the long term outcome.

Boy's early sexual experiences with adults are even less researched than female experiences. Landis (1956) reported that 30 per cent of male students who completed questionnaires reported at least one experience with an adult, and 84 per cent of these were homosexual approaches. More recently, Finkelhor (1979) found that nine per cent of another sample of male American students said that they had had sexual experiences with an adult when they were children, and again most of these experiences were of homosexual approaches. Some paedophiles are predominantly or exclusively interested in boys rather than girls, and there is evidence suggesting that boys, particularly older boys, may be often willing participants (O'Carroll 1980, Taylor 1981, Wilson and Cox 1983). However, the following incident, described by one of our interviewed respondents, in which an exhibitionist approached her when she was 13 and in the company of a boy two years older, suggests that boys as well as girls can sometimes be disturbed by unexpected sexual approaches:

> I was going down an alley way with David, my best friend's brother on the way to the youth club. It was about 7 p.m. and this man (in his twenties) leapt out and flashed us, but mostly at him. David started screaming. David backed against the wall and kept screaming and screaming as the man went towards him. It was very high pitched. David was shaking and crying and crying. He was absolutely petrified. I just stood there. The man ran off. The man was erect. It was the first time I'd seen it - it was a bit of a shock seeing this great thing sticking out. But I wasn't scared because I ended up comforting David because he was crying so. I wasn't terribly upset because I

had to handle my friend's brother. I had to tell his mother. She was quite hard and told David to stop crying and left him to get over it on his own. Susan [the girl-friend] was more sympathetic.

The results of this small exploratory study confirm that sexual contacts between female children and male adults are far more prevalent than generally realised, but that although common, such contacts are by no means always inconsequential. Unhappy childhood, early onset of overt sexual behaviour and adult sexual dissatisfaction were all more prevalent among the women who recalled such experiences. Future research will need to investigate further the meaning of these associations.

Part II
Socio-legal problems of male homosexuals in Britain

N. L. THOMPSON, D. J. WEST AND T. P. WOODHOUSE

10 Introduction

Since the decriminalisation of consensual homosexual acts between male adults in private, which took place in 1967, there
has been no diminution of the number of persons guilty of the
offence of indecency between males (638 in 1962, 1,183* in
1972, 1,237* in 1982 - the last two asterisked figures including a few who were officially cautioned, but without prosecution) (Home Office 1983). Apart from their continuing
vulnerability to prosecution, homosexual males still suffer,
according to some commentators, from various forms of social
and legal discrimination - in housing, in employment, in lia-
bility to blackmail and assault and in confrontations with the
police (Crane 1982). It could be that such complaints are
exaggerated through the well known tendency of unpopular min-
orities to develop a hypersensitivity to slights and unfair
treatment. Gay rights propagandists are particularly scathing
about the allegedly hostile attitudes and unfair practices of
the British police (Galloway 1983). These are said to include
verbal and physical intimidation in police cells, techniques
of entrapment in public lavatories, neglect of complaints of
criminal victimisation when the individual is known to be
homosexual, unnecessary raids on clubs, saunas and private
parties, spiteful revelations to families or employers of the
sexual orientation of men who have cooperated with police enquiries and exaggerated testimony during trial hearings. The
present investigation was an attempt to obtain some indication
of the nature and extent of the legal and social problems

encountered by male homosexuals in the community. We sought to find out, by systematic questioning of a sample of men who identified themselves as homosexuals, the variety of situations in which they find themselves at a disadvantage as a consequence of their orientation and the frequency and circumstances of their confrontations with police and other authorities.

Because we were obviously concerned to delve into the problematic aspects of homosexuality, some subjects felt that we were in danger of presenting homosexual living in an unfavourable light. We tried to guard against this by asking questions about contentment as well as discontent, and by balancing the numbers of problems described against the frequent reports of an absence of significant problems.

11 The questionnaire enquiry

METHOD

The enquiry was conducted initially by questionnaire, and then
by more detailed follow up interviews. Most of the interviews
took place in the subjects' own homes, with no third party
present. A pilot questionnaire was tried out on volunteers in
order to improve the comprehensibility and coverage of the
final version. The questionnaire asked about general background features, such as marital status, education, occupation,
age and birthplace, as well as about specific problems, such
as questioning by police in situations related to homosexual
behaviour and prosecutions for homosexual offences. There
were also questions asking whether, as a consequence of their
homosexuality, subjects had been criticised or rejected by
relatives or friends, had employment or housing difficulties,
or been physically assaulted or blackmailed.

The questionnaire was distributed by Dr Thompson through
social, political and religious gay organisations (either following talks or by making use of their mailing lists), through
the friendship networks of individual volunteers, and in response to enquiries from persons who had seen references to
the study in Gay News and Capital Gay. In order to guarantee
anonymity the questionnaire was posted to or taken away by the
respondent for completion in private and a stamped addressed
envelope was provided for its return. The distribution of the

questionnaires was in no way directed towards persons suspected of having problems. There was no means of knowing how
many of the questionnaires accepted for distribution to
friends were actually passed on, but more than half of the
total produced and distributed were returned completed.

A sample of homosexuals representative of the total population is virtually unobtainable. The method used in this study
inevitably resulted in a considerable over-representation of
young men and men with superior education. Nevertheless, the
questionnaire did reach men from a wide range of backgrounds,
partly because a deliberate effort was made to select some
volunteers with friendship groups different from those of the
majority of the sample. Of those who answered the question
'Where did you hear of this survey?' 101 said they had heard
of the enquiry from a friend, 272 through various gay groups
(including 89 from religious groups such as the Gay Christian
Movement), 38 from newspaper citations and 13 from miscellaneous sources.

COMPOSITION OF THE SAMPLE

A total of 443 usable questionnaires were returned by males.
On each individual item there were always a few who failed to
supply an answer. A small minority from females or persons of
unspecified sex were disregarded. The great majority of respondents (88.4 per cent of 437 who replied) said they had
'never married', 2.1 per cent said they were married and 9.6
per cent had been married but were separated, divorced or widowed. The age distribution, shown in Table 11.1, indicates
that over half were under 35.

The sample was heavily overweighted by men of superior education. Of 425 who gave the information, 64.9 per cent had at
least one university degree or were on a university course,
12.7 per cent had 'A' levels or further educational or professional qualifications without a university degree, 22.4 per
cent had no educational qualifications beyond 'O' levels.
Only 10.4 per cent (of 424) had completed their full time education before 16. In view of national trends, one might have
expected fewer with university qualifications among the older
respondents, but the distribution of educational levels was
actually similar in each age category.

The usual occupations (of 417 who gave classifiable responses) were roughly categorised as follows: professional,
managerial executive - 30.2 per cent; other white collar -
58.3 per cent; skilled manual - six per cent; unskilled manual

- 3.1 per cent; self employed - 1.4 per cent; never employed -
one per cent. (There were 10.4 per cent currently unemployed).

Nearly all were indigenous British; 91.2 per cent (of 424)
were born in the UK, and 42.6 per cent (of 423) were living in
the London area; the majority of the remaining respondents
were living in the southern counties of England.

Table 11.1
Age distribution of questionnaire respondents

Age	No.	%
15-24	73	16.6
25-34	162	36.8
35-44	94	21.4
45-54	54	12.3
55 and over	57	13.0
Total	440	100.0
No information	3	-

PROBLEMS REPORTED BY QUESTIONNAIRE RESPONDENTS

Of the total of 443 respondents, 34 (7.7 per cent) reported
having been at some time convicted of an offence connected
with homosexuality and a further 11 (2.5 per cent) said they
had been prosecuted but not found guilty. In addition, another 104 (23.5 per cent) had been questioned by the police
for some behaviour linked with homosexuality. A majority of
66.4 per cent reported never having had any of these problems.

With a male population at risk of a conviction for homosexual behaviour estimated at about a million, a national an-
nual incidence of first convictions in the thousands, and a
period of maximum exposure to risk of perhaps 40 years or more,
a prevalence rate of one in 13 men with a conviction history
was not as out of the way as at first sight it might appear.

Ten behavioural items were listed on the questionnaire. Table 11.2 shows the percentages of respondents who claimed to have been questioned, prosecuted or convicted for each of these. It can be seen that on each item a small proportion of respondents, mostly around six per cent, recorded no answer. From information provided at follow up interviews it was found that the usual reason for leaving a space blank was that the respondent had never had any such experience but had omitted to put a tick in the column headed 'never'.

The replies showed that loitering, soliciting and sexual activity in public places accounted for most of the confrontations with the police. It is of interest to note that the percentages of our sample who reported a prosecution for sexual activity in public (3.4 per cent), offences involving minors (1.1 per cent) and soliciting (4.3 per cent) were roughly similar to the corresponding percentages of persons arrested (five per cent, two per cent and five per cent) obtained from a sample of male homosexuals interviewed many years ago by Westwood (1960, p.137). His sample had been collected in a not dissimilar fashion, largely by the 'snowball' method, in which initial contacts recruited friends and friends of friends. As in this study, Westwood's sample was inevitably overweighted with younger men and men from the higher educational grades.

The reporting of prosecutions and convictions by our questionnaire respondents was checked against the detailed accounts given by those who were subsequently interviewed. The information was found to be very substantially consistent. Only two of the 30 interviewed men who described having been prosecuted or convicted had omitted mention of the fact on the questionnaire. The common place legal charges of importuning and indecency between males had been somewhat indiscriminately registered on the questionnaire as loitering, soliciting or sexual activity in public. Prosecutions for obstructing the police, connected with gay marches and groups congregated outside gay bars, were sometimes not mentioned on the questionnaire and sometimes listed under 'being in a gay pub or sauna'. One man who registered a conviction for importuning on his questionnaire explained at interview that although arrested and charged he had failed to respond to a summons to the court, but that no action had been taken against him on that account, although he was subsequently convicted of more serious, non-sexual offences.

As can be seen from Table 11.3, both convictions and confrontations with the police were distinctly less common among those of superior education. There were no acquittals among

100

Table 11.2

Numbers of men questioned, charged or convicted for various behaviours

Behaviour	Never questioned by police for this behaviour		Questioned by police but not charged		Charged but not convicted		Convicted		Total who answered question (=100%)
	No.	%	No.	%	No.	%	No.	%	No.
Being in a gay pub, club or sauna	365	85.9	57	13.4	-	-	3	0.7	425
Showing affection in public	396	94.7	21	5.0	1	0.2	-	-	418
Group sex in a private house	411	98.8	3	0.7	2	0.5	-	-	416
Sex with someone in the military	400	95.5	16	3.8	-	-	3	0.7	419
Loitering near a public lavatory or other gay place	333	78.6	76	17.9	5	1.2	10	2.4	424
Soliciting for gay sex	380	90.9	20	4.8	2	0.5	16	3.8	418
Sexual activity in public	382	91.8	20	4.8	2	0.5	12	2.9	416
Sex with someone under 21 but over 16 years	402	96.9	10	2.4	-	-	3	0.7	415
Sex with someone under 16	408	98.8	3	0.7	1	0.2	1	0.2	413
Possession of gay pornography.	398	96.6	12	2.9	1	0.2	1	0.2	412

Table 11.3

Prevalence of prosecutions for homosexual offences by educational background

	No qualification beyond 'O' level		'A' level etc.		University degree		Unclassified or unknown
	No.	%	No.	%	No.	%	No.
Questioned by police but not prosecuted	40	42.1	16	29.6	54	19.6	2
Charged, not convicted	–	–	2	3.7)	9	3.3	1
Convicted	11	11.6	7	13.0	13	4.7	3
No police contact	44	46.3	29	53.7	200	72.4	12
Total in educational group (N)	95	100.0	54	100.0	276	100.0	18

the least educated group, whereas 3.3 per cent of those with a degree had been charged and acquitted, but the figures were too small for this to be a statistically significant difference. Evidently, if the sample had been less skewed towards the better educated, there would have been a higher prevalence of conviction histories.

Twelve of the 34 respondents who reported having been convicted said they had been convicted for more than one type of behaviour, and 47 of the 112 questioned by the police had been questioned for more than one type of behaviour. The questionnaire did not ask specifically for the total number of occasions convicted, but evidently a first conviction considerably increased the likelihood of further convictions.

Apart from the ten questions about the specific behaviours listed in Table 11.2, which might have led to prosecution, the questionnaire left a space for 'Other problems with the courts or police because of your homosexuality?'. This produced a mention by 26 respondents of some confrontation with police not otherwise covered. A commonly cited circumstance was being questioned about their homosexuality when the initial reason for contact with the police was for something different, as in the following examples.

> During a search of my home for cannabis I was questioned about gay campaigning material and pornography [found on the premises].

> Once I was stopped by the police. They found gay liberation leaflets in my bag and were verbally abusive.

> I was stopped by the police once with a friend in a car in London. We were asked whether we were homosexual. Our names and addresses were taken. The general attitude of the officer was very provocative.

> I was involved with the police when I disappeared overnight and did not contact my parents.

In some instances the reported confrontations were obviously considered by the respondents as a form of mild harassment by the police:

> I used to be stopped and breathalysed on leaving a gay club in Bedfordshire. The police sometimes made remarks such as "Have you got a car full of queers?".

> I was questioned in the street by plain clothes police officers because I was wearing a handkerchief in my back pocket. [Handkerchiefs in that position being used by some gay men as an indicator of sexual preference]

I was cautioned by the police about disseminating information on gay groups and switchboards [i.e. telephone helping services] via stickers and cards.

Other minor difficulties mentioned included being 'moved on'
from the environs of gay pubs at closing time, being questioned in the course of enquiries concerning crimes in which
they were in no way involved, and being treated dismissively
on making a complaint to the police:

I was being harassed by silent telephone calls during two
separate periods. On one occasion I 'phoned the police.
They were less than pleasant when I said I was openly gay
[as a teacher] at school, suggesting that I had asked for
problems etc. They refused to take down details and so on.

More frequent and detailed examples of these kinds of complaints were obtained later in the course of follow up interviews.

Eight of the questionnaire respondents used this part of the
form to record unsolicited general comments about the police:

I am a professional man with - I hope - rational and un-
prejudiced views. But as far as the police go I have
absolutely no confidence in their willingness to aid gay
people impartially. Quite literally, it is looking for
trouble to involve the police in any way if it is a gay-
related issue.

Despite my regular professional contacts with [the police]
I feel totally alienated from them and everything they
stand for.

In contrast to these examples of hostility, two questionnaire respondents commented on the fact that the police had
not arrested them on occasions when there was ample justification for doing so:

On one occasion the police turned a blind eye when I was
seen having sex in a cottage [i.e. public lavatory].

Another respondent reported that the police had become aware
of a sexual relationship he was having with a gay man under 21
through the young man's diaries, but to his surprise they did
not even question him about it.

Further examples of the discretionary 'blind eye' were described in the subsequent interviews.

A surprisingly large number (29.2 per cent of 425) answered

'yes' to the question 'Have you ever been physically attacked by a person or gang of people who did this because they thought you were gay?'. (Although not specifically asked to do so, ten respondents reported having been attacked more than once, but second or subsequent attacks were not counted in the following figures). Of those attacked, 73.4 per cent (91 of 124) reported that the assailants were strangers or gangs and 15.3 per cent (19 of 124) said they were 'casual sex partners' (which included some 'hustlers'). The remaining attacks were by persons otherwise known to the victim. About one in four said they had reported the attack to the police. Asked about the reaction of the police, only one in three described it in favourable terms. Physical attacks were reported less often by respondents with a university degree (23.6 per cent of 276) than by those with 'A' levels etc. (44.4 per cent of 54) or by those with no more than 'O' levels (36.8 per cent of 95). The difference according to educational level was statistically significant (χ^2 = 13.0 with 2° freedom, p = 0.0015). As many as 46 respondents said they had been 'blackmailed' but it was only at subsequent interviews that it became possible to determine what this meant.

Substantial numbers said they had lost friends or been crit-icised or rejected by parents, family members or others on ac-count of their homosexuality, or had experienced unpleasant remarks from persons at work. Smaller numbers reported hous-ing problems, such as harassment by landlords, or dismissal from employment. Table 11.4 lists the responses to these items.

Respondents were asked, in an open ended question, to des-cribe other housing or employment problems not already covered. This elicited very few specific examples of discrimination in employment. As in other sections of the questionnaire, the problem most frequently cited in this context was the awkward-ness of concealment:

Only the practical necessity that I conceal [my homosex-uality] which I regard as disturbing.

Staying partly closeted, because I knew my boss was anti-gay.

Many respondents mentioned their suspicions that they had failed to get jobs or promotion because it was known or thought they might be gay, but few were able to be sure:

I was selected for a job as a junior hospital doctor and later the offer was withdrawn. The reason was not stated but I suspect my homosexuality became known to the doctor concerned.

Table 11.4
Numbers of respondents who endorsed various problems
listed on the questionnaire

Social Problem	Yes	No	Uncertain (Believe homosexuality involved but not sure)	No reply or not applicable (e.g. homosexuality not known to person(s) in question)
Lost a hetero-sexual female friend	42	290	30	81
Lost a hetero-sexual male friend	100	224	47	72
Criticised by mother	105	195	17	126
Mother said she did not want to see you again	18	294	2	129
Criticised by father	71	184	10	178
Father said he did not want to see you again	17	250	1	175
Criticised by other family members	70	236	14	123
Other family members said they did not want to see you again	21	289	3	130
Shunned by members of your church	30	188	12	213
Shunned by neighbours (who were not close friends)	39	248	21	135
Refused a housing loan	5	307	1	130
Evicted from a flat or house	11	345	4	83
Harassed by landlord or landlady	19	337	10	77
Sacked for homosexuality	20	362	14	47
Unpleasant remarks from co-workers	109	261	29	44
Difficulties with boss, but not sacked	51	314	17	61

I have occasionally been asked at interviews questions which, I believe, were designed to elicit a response about homosexuality in a roundabout way, e.g. "Are you averse to female company?".

I seemed to be doing well in my probationary year until I mentioned my homosexuality. Then I kept failing probationary period (twice). I left teaching. At the time I thought I was just not coping with the job, looking back, I am suspicious.

Respondents who were teachers or clergymen or who worked with young people often mentioned the special difficulties of being homosexual in their particular jobs:

Anyone in teaching (especially in the past) has to be extremely circumspect about revealing homosexual tendencies. Concealment seemed to me the only safe policy. Age of students seems not to matter.

As a Church of England priest (parish) considerable "crisis of confidence" around time when my homosexuality was learnt of.

Most of the complaints were directed against heterosexual work colleagues who were disapproving, but some respondents thought that gay colleagues keen to conceal their own orientation could also cause difficulties:

I have a slight suspicion that at one time someone senior to me, who I later found out was gay, made himself difficult to me because he thought I might be so, and rumble his gayness.

Only a few examples of direct discrimination in housing were volunteered:

A former lodger in my (own) house told me after he'd left that, had I told him of my homosexuality when he first came to live here, he would never have come!

One owner refused to sell her house to known gays (myself and my lover).

Several respondents mentioned a problem with obtaining mortgages for gay couples, although others mentioned that they had experienced no difficulty:

I got my mortgage because of a gay contact in a building society.

It was not surprising, considering the relatively superior social class of most of the respondents, that few mentioned

the special difficulties encountered by gay men trying to secure accomodation in public housing:

> As a gay man I am registered as "single" (i.e. waiting to
> be married) therefore I have had to wait longer in the
> private sector paying high rents. Only recently have some
> London Boroughs and some housing societies not discrimin-
> ated against gay couples.

It became apparent from subsequent interviews that most of
our respondents were living either alone or with lovers or
with friends who were also gay, rarely among heterosexuals.
One respondent volunteered a possible reason for this:

> I shared with two other men in one place, who couldn't
> cope with me because I was gay as they thought people
> would think they were. They were difficult with all my
> friends (straight and gay) but not too bad to me. I moved
> as I thought it was too silly.

There were two open ended questions asking respondents to
'specify' any 'other social difficulties' and 'other instances
of discrimination or problems' not already covered. Unlike
the question on 'other problems with police or courts', which
elicited relatively few comments, these questions produced
replies from 143 respondents.

The most frequently mentioned problem, cited by 46 respondents, was the necessity to be discreet about their homosexual
orientation. For example:

> Difficulty in being forced to lead a double life and to
> conform; although if challenged I would not deny it.

> My life has to be in two separate compartments owing to my
> family and straight friends and relations and my gay "fam-
> ily" and friends. My business life of course falls into
> the first section.

> Maintaining "straight" appearances among heterosexual
> friends.

A few men admitted that they used deliberate ruses to hide
their sexual orientation:

> [Problems of] who to take to the office party etc. - solved
> because I have several close female friends...

> No one on board [this naval vessel] knows that I am in the
> Gay Christian Movement, my subs. are paid by standing or-
> der through the bank. [But] should I ever be questioned
> by security I should therefore be able to say I am no risk
> because I have been open.

Some respondents emphasised that they disliked secrecy but were forced into it because of the difficulties caused when they tried to be more open:

> In [my home town] I always felt I had to be discreet with neighbours and friends of the family, to avoid causing my parents embarrassment...In my present job as resident head porter I again have to be secretive in case of complaints. This enforced discretion annoys me intensely.

> The chief problem...is the lack of opportunity to assist or advise those for whom I am pastorally responsible [as a lecturer in a theological college]. Heterosexuals tend to avoid close personal contact because of prejudice: homosexuals tend to avoid [me] through fear of drawing attention to themselves.

> [College] life is difficult because I'm so open and therefore teased; but it can be fun as mostly the taunts are in fun anyway.

> Perhaps a slight stand-offishness by business associates who I believe recognised me as a homosexual and felt uncomfortable or even threatened.

> I don't look gay. One good female friend asked me why so many of my friends were gay...I told her it was because I was gay. The poor woman could not cope or initially believe it, and has avoided me ever since.

> I was studying for matriculation as a preliminary to training for the priesthood. It was then that I fell in love for the first time. Naively, I told my vicar who was also my spiritual director. As a result he withdrew his sponsorship and I was unable to go forward to the Selection Board.

> [As a student] in Sixth Form College generally shunned and a figure to laugh at by pupils and even one lecturer, who contributed to anti-gay jokes - though behind my back.

Many of those who mentioned encountering difficulties when they were openly gay also commented that their relationships with lovers were not afforded the same consideration or recognition as would be analogous heterosexual relationships:

> I have been criticised by my partner's mother because she does not acknowledge my right to be involved in all his business. (I feel she would prefer me to act as a friend rather than as a member of the family).

> Not always having gay partners, even of long-standing, recognised as being as important to me as the spouses of heterosexuals [are to them].

Unable to "marry" my partner. Not perceived as a couple
in consequence. Not considered as his next of kin - as
when he was seriously ill in hospital [when I was] not
contacted or admitted to see him.

When you have a [homosexual] relationship, there is a lot
of heterosexual pressure - rather family pressure - to
break it up. No invitations for your partner, snide remarks etc.

Some men made the point that the fact that they had few difficulties of the kind listed in the questionnaire might be
attributed to their exercise of discretion:

Social difficulties tend not to arise where one's homosexuality is not publicly known.

[My] relative lack of difficulties is of course due to the
discretion (i.e. concealment - also sometimes good manners)
which I have observed.

Specific examples of social discrimination were quoted by 37
respondents. Their complaints included discrimination by the
tax system, by employers in the educational system, by political organisations and, most common of all, inappropriate
treatment by the medical profession (of which ten cases were
cited):

A hospital colleague in general practice told some
patients he didn't think I was a fit person to consult [as
a physician] as I was homosexual.

My G.P. told me that the man I was living with (and who is
still my partner) was homosexual and therefore "dangerous"
for me.

Hostile reception at a V.D. clinic.

Lectured by doctor recently. Told me homosexuality was
only a personal choice and I ought to pull myself together
and go "straight".

My parents and school had me admitted into two mental hos-
pitals to change my sexuality. I spent four and a half
months in hospital, at age 15, during which time psych-
iatrists endeavoured to "persuade" me into heterosexuality.
The experience was very powerful and distressing at that
age.

At least ten men referred to the emotional damage they felt
they had experienced through unsuccessful efforts to suppress
their homosexuality:

I have a learned shyness and introvertness which I

110

attribute to feeling I always had to repress my feelings.

Hiding one's real feelings - playing the games of pretence (very probably unnecessarily!). Result - the building up of a reserve, opting out of some situations etc. I think I was socially damaged.

The problems of coming to terms with their homosexuality was alluded to by 11 respondents. This was a topic that recurred in the more detailed descriptions at later interviews. It is probably something that affects a high proportion of male homosexuals. Among those who cited this on their question-naires, the problem seemed to have been more persistent than usual:

Adapting to society and accepting my own homosexuality in a society which doesn't. This took very many years.

Until I was 50 I did not really accept my condition, and until then regarded it as a serious sin against Christian morality. I found the double life I lived as a priest under the Christian ethic and my own orientation intoler-able.

I think perhaps the biggest problems are before you come to terms with your sexuality and you believe the popular mis-conceptions of what homosexuality is. I found this caused a lot of worry and mental turmoil.

Lack of support and help when I was "coming out". No sex education about homosexuality at school, negative images, derogatory language etc. Coming to terms with myself was a long, painful and traumatic experience.

Although many comments referred to the unfavourable and pre-judiced attitudes of heterosexuals towards gays, others were equally expressive of a dislike of 'straights' on the part of some of these homosexual respondents who seemed to share the same 'them and us' mentality for which the heterosexual major-ity were so often being blamed:

I don't socialise more than is necessary with straight people.

[I have a] general dislike of straight men - although I don't regard this as a difficulty.

As time goes on [heterosexuals] become child orientated and you find you have little in common, and frankly they are boring.

12 The interviewed sample

THE COMPOSITION OF THE SAMPLE

A detachable sheet was included with the questionnaire request-
ing the respondents to volunteer for an interview so that we
could explore social and legal issues in greater depth. A
total of 297 men (67 per cent of the original sample) completed this sheet with a contact address or telephone number
and returned it either together with the questionnaire or in a
separate envelope to avoid putting their name with the papers
carrying intimate particulars.

An effort was made to contact as many as possible of the men
who were willing to be seen who had reported being charged or
arrested for an offence connected with homosexuality. In addition, others who had not been charged were interviewed in
order to obtain a comparison group. These were selected
partly on grounds of easy availability, but also with a view
to the inclusion of sufficient men of the required age and
educational status to form a control group matched individually on both these variables with the men of the 'offender'
group. The interviewees were also chosen so as to include a
substantial number who had been questioned by the police but
not prosecuted. Interviewing ceased when a total of 100 had
been seen.

The interviewed sample consisted of 30 men who had been

charged with at least one offence, a control group of 30
matched with the 'offenders' on age and educational status and
a further 40, making up the total of 100. Each of the authors
carried out roughly a third of the interviews.

As in the total sample of questionnaire respondents, the
interviewed men included a large number with a university degree or its equivalent (52) and only 23 who had no more than
'O' levels or the equivalent.

Given the additional information available from personal interviews, it was possible to classify the respondents by occupation according to the Registrar General's categorisation
(see Table 12.1).

Table 12.1
Occupational categories of interviewed men
compared with UK population

	Interviewed sample		UK male Employed Population (1983)*	
	%		%	
Professional, managerial	20		31	
Other non-manual	45		12	
Skilled manual	15)		)	
	)		)	
Semi-skilled manual	10)	30	)	54
	)		)	
Unskilled manual	5)		)	
Never employed or unclassified	5		2	

* Office of Population Censuses and Surveys (1984)

It can be seen that the sample has relatively few manual
workers and an excess of non-manual workers, but no excess in
the highest professional or managerial grade, such as might
have been expected of a sample containing so many of superior
educational attainment. In the general population less than
one per cent of males in either skilled or semi-skilled manual

113

occupations have a university degree, compared with 20 per cent and ten per cent respectively among our interviewed group. In the non-manual occupations other than professional and managerial, only 12 per cent of the population have a degree compared with 62 per cent of the 45 interviewees who were so employed (Office of Population Censuses and Surveys 1982).

One probable reason for the poor correlation between education and occupational achievement in our sample may be that unmarried status, and the fairly open homosexual life style favoured by many, are not conducive to career orientated jobs or appointments to high level management. Comments from some of those interviewed suggesting failure to obtain promotion because of their homosexuality supports this explanation.

Almost all of the interviewed men, 97, acknowledged that they were either exclusively or else predominantly homosexual and only insignificantly heterosexual. Only two endorsed the category of predominantly homosexual but significantly heterosexual, and only one said that he was equally homosexual and heterosexual, although he had been convicted of a homosexual offence.

Asked about their 'feelings' as opposed to their sexual practices, the corresponding figures were 96, two, and two.

The great majority, 89, had never been married; six were divorced; five were separated or living apart from their wives (two of whom had contracted marriages of convenience to enable foreign women to remain in the country).

Most of the interviewed men were very confirmed homosexuals; 84 of them gave a negative and often emphatically negative response to the question whether, imagining such a thing were possible, they would have liked to have received some simple treatment at birth to ensure a heterosexual development. Asked whether they would like such treatment today, 95 said 'No', only two 'Yes', with three 'Uncertain'.

Another indication that homosexual orientation was deeply entrenched in most of the respondents was that a substantial proportion said that they had suspected they were gay from a quite early age, 43 before reaching the age of 13, of whom 29 had suspected it by age 11. As the following examples show, those who had been aware of their homosexuality in boyhood, usually on account of their attraction to other boys, sometimes sought contacts with adults as well, but these contacts were nearly always a result, not a cause, of their inclinations, as in the following examples [1]:

He found himself interested in other boys' bodies when he was aged eight or nine and he had some sex experiences at that time. At age 11 or 12 he was turned on a lot by the masturbatory activities of his schoolfellows, but he felt guilty about it.

From the age of ten he had an obvious attraction to other boys in his all male boarding school. He realised his feelings were different from other boys, but he wasn't disturbed by it. He just slid gradually into thinking of himself as homosexual. He was never interested in or tried to have sex with women.

He first suspected he might be gay at age 13 through physical attraction to other boys. His family's attitude and religion made him feel guilty about it. By age 16 he was visiting lavatories weekly. By age 17 he realised he was interested only in men and not in going off with girls like his friends.

Born in 1905, this respondent explained that the subject of homosexuality was never discussed at the time he was growing up. At age 15, while still at school, he started visiting lavatories every day and would have sex there, but he did not know what a homosexual was and did not realise he was one until he was 30. By then he felt it was a part of his nature. 'One was born that way'.

He had sex contacts with other boys from age seven. At the time he thought it was fun. Later he felt isolated because of his homosexuality.

He became sexually involved with another boy at school when he was 14. He felt emotionally about it, but it was purely sexual on the other boy's part. He assumed at the time that a lot of others felt as he did, but he knew he had to keep it quiet from parents and the like.

From age 13 or 14 he knew he was gay from his attraction to other boys. He felt desperately frustrated because he had no outlet; he could not find others who felt the same. Being bookish he looked it up, but all the reading was 'terribly negative'. At age 16 to 17 he began to hang around a local station lavatory. He liked to get picked up and fussed over by older males.

He was about 12 when he first had sex with another boy. From age 15 to 18 he had a sexual affair with an older, married man, with whom he became very emotionally involved. At the same time he was also having sex with girls. He felt guilty at first, but by age 20 onwards he became more reconciled to 'being himself', that is homosexual. He subsequently lived with a lover for 16 years, until bereaved.

He was aware of sexual attraction and fascination to boys in childhood. At age 11 he was fantasising about male teachers and other boy pupils. At age 12 he started frequent visits to public lavatories.

The following example, the only one of those interviewed who said he was completely bisexual, was exceptional in mentioning sex contacts with older males as a reason for first suspecting he had homosexual inclinations:

The respondent said he was 'brought into it' at about 11 through having casual sex encounters with adults he met - usually in public lavatories. He liked going 'cottaging'. At age 14 he went into a gay pub and felt 'at home'. It never worried him having gay sex. He just carried on with normal life regardless.

ACCEPTANCE AND OPENNESS

Because the sample included so many who had been contacted through their affiliations to gay organisations, it was unsurprising that expressions of belief in living an openly gay life style were common. Nevertheless, from replies to specific questions, it seemed that a significant proportion had found it necessary to engage in concealments of various kinds, especially in relation to their family of origin. Moreover, reports of the reactions of others to the revelation of their homosexuality showed that there was sometimes good reason for concealment.

Of the 94 men whose mothers were alive and in contact with them when they reached adulthood, as many as 32 thought their mothers did not or might not know of their homosexuality. Of 76 who had fathers available, 37 said that they did not or might not know. This was, in itself, a sign of considerable reserve on the topic within families.

Parents' reactions on first being told or finding out about their sons' homosexuality were often negative, although some became more accepting later. Typical examples were:

I told her five years ago. She took it better than I thought she would, resigned to it more than accepting. She never discusses it now.

She reacted badly when I told her. She has started to

116

mellow a bit since, but she doesn't discuss it.

Some reactions were violently hostile:

> He was told by my school [of my homosexuality] when I was
> 15. He remained completely hostile to the end, and would
> never allow the subject to be raised.

> He has a horror of the subject, has shut his mind to it.
> He is very anti-gay. Never speaks of it.

> I told her when I was 26. She didn't speak to me for two
> years after.

Of the 94 men whose mothers were still around when they had
reached age 20, there were 62 who were said definitely to know
about their sons' homosexuality, and 56 men said that they had
told or categorically admitted the fact to their mothers. The
initial reactions, when these were described sufficiently to
be categorised, were 34 negative, 15 neutral and seven positive. Of the 76 available fathers, 39 were said definitely to
know of their sons' homosexuality, and 33 men said they had
volunteered or admitted the fact to their fathers. The initial reactions described were categorised as 18 negative, 15
neutral and three positive.

There was some softening of parental attitudes with lapse of
time. Among the mothers still available who knew about their
sons' homosexuality, 16 were said to have present attitudes
that could be described as favourable, 18 neutral and 13 negative, and of 30 fathers, seven were presently favourable, 18
neutral and seven negative.

The reported attitudes of siblings included more that could
be classed as positive. Of the 78 men who had one or more
siblings, 21 said that their siblings did not know or may not
have known of their homosexuality. Of the 53 men who described the reactions of siblings who did know, 17 said that
all were positive, 12 that all were neutral, eight all negative and 16 varied, that is different siblings having different attitudes.

A majority of 81 men said that all or most of their close
male friends were homosexual. Asked about close male friends
who were heterosexual, only 51 claimed to have any. Of these,
36 said that they had been open about their homosexuality to
their heterosexual male friends, 12 had not and three gave no
clear answer. More of the men, 73, said they had one or more
close heterosexual female friends: 60 had been open to these
friends, 11 not so and two gave no information. Describing
the attitudes of close heterosexual male friends who knew

117

about their sexuality, 17 said they were uniformly positive, seven uniformly neutral, three uniformly negative and six varied. Among men with close female heterosexual friends who knew, 40 described uniformly positive attitudes, nine uniformly neutral, four uniformly negative and three varied. Clearly, willingness to confide and chances of an accepting reaction were commoner in relation to female than to male heterosexual friends.

Asked about their situation at work, 83 had someone in the role of boss or supervisor and 39 said their boss did not know of their homosexuality or else they were unsure if he knew. Describing bosses who did know about them, 23 reported a positive attitude, nine a neutral one and five a negative one. A substantial number, 41, had themselves told or admitted to their boss that they were homosexual. A rather larger number, 54, had been frank with colleagues at work, but ten said that they had taken positive steps to avoid their sexuality becoming known at their place of work. Describing the attitudes of colleagues who did know about them, 21 described uniformly positive attitudes, 13 uniformly neutral, two uniformly negative and eight varied. Asked whether they had ever been dismissed or failed to secure promotion on account of their homosexuality, 27 said they thought so and a further nine suspected so.

As the following examples show, these crude statistics embrace a wide range of experiences, reflecting conflicting pressures towards openness and concealment and a variety of responses from family and friends:

When he was 15 he was caught at school having sex with another boy. His parents were informed and also the social services. In addition he had been having contact with older men in a park. His parents were very hostile and sent him to a psychiatrist for aversion treatment. He thought he would be happy to be gay, and the psychiatrist was understanding, but his parents 'blew up' at the idea. He was made to leave school prematurely and his freedom was severely curtailed. He wanted to be able to have sex with a girl, and tried to do so, but it did not work out.

Right up to his death his father remained hostile to the subject and would never allow it to be raised. His mother, however, changed completely after a couple of years and became supportive, but his elder brother has remained permanently antagonistic. He has not confided in his boss, or in heterosexual male friends – because he has none – and he has not told his co-workers, although some of them got to know by various means. He has one older female heterosexual friend who has known about him from the beginning and was very supportive during the troubles with his parents. Now aged 26 he has been living with his present lover for eight years.

This respondent's parents were dead. His father died too early to have known. He thinks his mother may have suspected, but he never told her. His brothers may have 'drawn their own conclusions', but he never discussed it openly with them or with his boss or colleagues at work. Earlier in his life he had given up a naval career because he wanted to have a more private life. One had to be so discreet in the navy and it was difficult to be so living among a large body of men. He feels at some disadvantage because 'one is accepted by a limited circle of the rest of the population'.

When, at age 28, he had informed his mother she was taken aback only because he had taken so long to tell her. He had no siblings and no father available to tell. He worked in local government and had told his boss and co-workers and experienced no problem as a result, save that some of his colleagues misunderstood because he said he does not come across as gay and does not fit their stereotype. In his late twenties, when an officer in the RAF, he had been working on high security projects, for which he had been given clearance. He was having an affair, fairly openly, with a male civilian. He decided to tell his C.O. about it, as that seemed less risky and more dignified than allowing it to be discovered. He was interviewed for five hours in a formal but friendly way by Special Investigation Branch about his personal life. Their concern was with security and they wondered if he had come forward on account of blackmail. He was allowed to resign his commission.

This young man, who in the opinion of the interviewer sported obviously gay dress and manner, was working in a gay pub, where everyone knew him as a homosexual. He said he had no 'straight' friends and was quite content as he was - it suited him. At age 16 he had been caught by his mother in bed with another boy. She told him she already knew. She did not mind at all, and he used to take her with him to a gay club, which she liked. His father had 'a mental fit' at the first discovery and would not speak to him for months, but now just does not mention it and has accepted it.

This respondent, now aged 41, was an only child. His father died when he was 16, before he had become openly homosexual. He thinks his mother may suspect it as she often steers the conversation round to marriage, but he feels he can't tell her and steers her away from the subject whenever she brings it up. He thinks his boss knows, although they have never discussed it. He has been told to bring anyone he wants to office parties, but he feels he should not bring his lover. He has tried to cover up at work by talking about women and 'half acting' heterosexual. He has told one close heterosexual male friend, who proved accepting, but with female heterosexual friends it is never discussed.

At age 21 he took a lover to stay at his parental home. Seeing how close they were his mother confronted him and he told her he was gay. At the time she was very tearful and upset, but later she accepted it and talked about it. She told his father, who was furious, and although accepting it tacitly later would still never refer to it. He commented, 'It is difficult for my parents as I am an only child and they want grandchildren - a sore spot and I don't want to rub salt in the wound'. Outside the family he had become very open and involved in gay groups. All his friends of both sexes know he is gay, as do his boss and co-workers; 'If they don't know within a week they're thick. I don't try to pretend, I laugh at what I am'.

Clearly, there are considerable difficulties about being completely open and the comments at the interviews showed great variation in willingness or ability to reveal homosexuality to others. Each respondent was asked if he had let the following know about his homosexuality: mother, father, close heterosexual male friend, close heterosexual female friend, boss, or work colleagues - and 37 reported that they had told people from at least three of these six categories. The proportion reporting this degree of overtness was much higher among the younger men; 53.6 per cent (15 of 28) of respondents aged 30 or under; 38.3 per cent (18 of 47) of those aged 31 to 50; and only 16 per cent (four of 25) of those aged over 50. None of the youngest group, but three of the mid-range group and eight of the oldest group said they had never told anyone in any of the six categories.

It may be that openness about homosexuality has some tendency to decline with increasing age and social responsibilities, but the trend revealed by these interviews suggests a real difference between generations as greater public awareness of homosexuality makes concealment more difficult and perhaps less necessary.

Overtness was not related to educational level. Among those with no more than 'O' levels, 37.5 per cent were among the 37 'overt' respondents, compared with 33.3 per cent of the intermediate group and 38.5 per cent of the university group.

QUESTIONING BY POLICE

A substantial proportion of the respondents reported having
been questioned by the police in connection with homosexuality
other than on occasions that led to a charge being laid
against them: 29 men reported one such incident, ten remembered two, seven remembered three and two remembered more than
three.

The most frequent reason for questioning was being in or
near a lavatory or cruising area and coming under suspicion of
importuning or public indecency. Of the 48 first occasions of
questioning that were reported, 14 were in this category.
Other fairly frequent reasons were confrontations with police
outside a gay bar or in some other gay situation (seven instances) or queries about sex orientation in the course of investigation of a non-sexual offence (another seven instances).

The following examples were fairly typical:

He was in a lavatory which was being watched by uniformed
police in a car. They were timing people as they went in.
Two officers came into the lavatory and asked the six men who
were there to leave. They took names and addresses and
checked by radio to see if they were 'known'. He was asked
what he had been doing, but said that he had just been using
the lavatory normally. He was not charged with any offence.

He was questioned outside a gay bar, asked who he was and
what he was doing. The police were sneering, dismissive and
derogatory but not particularly unpleasant. He moved on feeling indignation and amusement.

When he was 16 a policeman saw him kissing goodbye to someone in the street. He was told not to do that. Nothing more
happened and he just went away.

He had two male lodgers staying with him. They were under
21, but he wasn't having sex with them. A cheque book was
stolen and the police were called. He was openly gay and
there were gay posters around the place. When the police came
they were not interested in the theft, only in his personal
life. He was questioned closely about his 'relations' with
the lodgers and how he had met them.

Although some of those questioned were obviously committing

121

offences at the time whey were not charged:

When serving in the RAF he was, as he said, well known as a communist rebel, and in addition he was having brief sex affairs with other airmen and there was gossip about that. As a result he was questioned very frequently by the military police, at one point several times a week, both on the subject of political affiliations and on sex relations. After some months of this he decided to buy himself out of the RAF, which he was allowed to do, but only after an unusual delay, which he thought was deliberate so that the authorities could go on questioning him. He was given normal discharge and an 'extremely good' character on his discharge papers.

When he was 19 the police raided the flat where he was living with a lover aged 25. They were searching for drugs, but discovered gay pornography. They threatened to arrest his lover for being with someone under age 21, but after continuing to threaten for some time they changed their minds.

At age 33 he was having a sex affair with a boy aged 15 whom he had at first thought was older. The boy ran away from home leaving behind a compromising letter from him which the parents found and took to the police. The police came to his flat and took him to the police station for questioning. They were abusive and frighteningly threatening and suggested that the boy might have been murdered. He denied having had anal sex with the boy, although that had happened often. The boy returned home soon after. No case was brought against him. Probably the boy did not admit that sex acts had taken place. It was an emotional as well as a sexual attachment that they had had.

Some of the respondents had become the subjects of police enquiries because their names had appeared in compromising address lists:

Six respondents had been questioned in the course of murder investigations. In three of the cases it seems that police were attempting to interview as many gay men as possible in a particular area. In two of the other three cases the police had questioned the respondents because their names had been found in address books. In one case the name may have been in the victim's address book and in the other it had been found in the address book of a suspect. In the sixth case the respondent was questioned about the murder of a young girl when his name was found on the Paedophile Information Exchange mailing list.

Three of these respondents described the police questioning in negative terms. One said the police were 'aggressive' and 'unpleasant'; another said they were 'somewhat harassing'. The third said he found the whole thing distasteful, and though he did say that the officer who was questioning him felt the same, he was moved to make a complaint about the incident. None of the other three respondents made any adverse comments about the police who questioned them, though one said that he was frightened. All six seemed to have cooperated with the enquiries and in fact one of the men went voluntarily to the station after the police telephoned him at work.

One respondent claimed he had been the victim of a malicious complaint by a nextdoor neighbour who disapproved of the fact that he was living with a lover. He was picked up by the police because she had said he had appeared dressed only in a blanket and exposed himself, which was untrue. He was heavily interrogated for two hours. The police clearly believed him guilty and claimed the story would appear in the papers unless he confessed. After this the police called at the house twice in the middle of the night; once to ask if a certain person was there; once to tell them to wind up the window of the car outside. He believed the real purpose was to harass him and his lover. The police had seen a gay novel he had with him when they picked him up for questioning. No charges were brought, but he and his lover moved away soon after.

PHYSICAL ATTACKS

A substantial proportion of those interviewed, 49 in all, reported having been physically attacked at least once in connection with their homosexuality, 13 recalled two attacks and four described three attacks. Of the total of 70 attacks, 21 were by an unknown assailant, 28 by two or more unknown assailants, 15 by a casual sex partner, two by a lover and five by persons not readily classifiable.

Only ten of the 70 attacks resulted in broken bones or an injury sufficient to require overnight hospitalisation, 16 produced cuts and bruises, but 44 caused no significant physical harm. Attacks in or near public lavatories accounted for 15 of the incidents, attacks in outdoor 'cruising' areas another eight and attacks in or near a gay pub another nine. The victim or a third party reported 19 of the incidents to the police. In seven instances their reaction was described as helpful or supportive, but in four cases they were said to have more or less ignored the complaint and in two cases to have been very negative or accusatory towards the complainant.

123

In a further six cases the information was inadequate to categorise the police response. It would seem that there was about an even chance of a complainant obtaining from the police a response he considered satisfactory.

The following examples illustrate the two most common circumstances in which assults took place, namely public behaviour or appearance suggestive of homosexuality, which attracted attention from disapproving observers, or casual sexual contacts with strangers whose reactions or motives are misjudged. Some incidents were quite serious, others trivial.

The respondent, then aged 20, was set upon by several men outside a gay club he had been visiting. He said his appearance was flamboyant at the time, which was presumably the reason why he was picked out to be attacked. He was badly hurt, sustaining a broken leg and being off work for two months. He went to the police about it. The officer asked if the complainant was gay and on being told 'yes' tore up the form he had been filling out.

Visiting a public lavatory around midnight the respondent was importuned by another man. At his invitation the man followed him out. The next he knew he was regaining consciousness and bleeding from the nose and back of the head, where he had been hit. He managed to get home. Nothing had been stolen, so theft did not seem to have been the motive. Next day he went to the police and told them he had been attacked in the street, but he did not explain that he had been 'cottaging'.

The respondent was at a tea party arranged by a gay students' group. They had a banner which made clear what they were. On leaving with a companion the two of them were assailed by a group of young men hurling stones and bottles at them. They hurried off, but were followed, running. They went to sit with some other people, but the stones continued to be thrown, so they walked further on and the assailants then disappeared. The respondent suffered no more than a slight bruise. The incident was reported to the police, who took the attitude that the gay tea party was a provocation.

The respondent, then aged about 40, had picked up a younger man in a gay bar and promised him some money for sex. When they got to his room the young man demanded more money than had been agreed and threatened him with a broken glass. The respondent explained, truthfully, that his wallet was in the car outside. When they went out into the street together to get it he was able to make his escape. A few days later they

124

met again in the same bar. The young man was quite friendly and even suggested coming back with him a second time. At no stage had he thought to complain to the police because in his job (teaching) he could not afford to have his homosexuality made known.

The subject was rather drunk at the time. On his way home he had to get off the bus because he felt ill and needed fresh air. He was resting on a bench when a man came along, saw he was drunk, and offered to help. They walked along together, the man helping to support him and giving the impression of being gay by seeming affectionate. He responded accordingly and the man led him to a dark place. The man took off his trousers and he did the same, but as soon as his own trousers were off he realised the man had been pretending. He was pushed over and kicked everywhere about his body. His money and watch were taken. The man ripped off his underwear, scratching his legs in the process, and then left. He got home, but was taken to hospital and the police were called. The man was identified, because someone had recognised him getting off the bus, and was arrested and charged. The police saw it as an ordinary assault and robbery, not an offence which occurred because of the victim's homosexuality.

The respondent, then aged 24, was leaving a gay bar in the company of three friends, one wearing a gay badge, when a group of young men outside started abusing them verbally. The friend with the gay badge started arguing back. He tried to get his friend to come away, but one of the men came up and punched him in the eye, then ran away. Some hours later he decided to go to the police and make a statement, explaining that he had been attacked because he was gay. The policeman adopted a neutral attitude. Some days later, because another witness had reported the same incident he was asked to return to the police station to look at some 'mug shots', but he could not identify any. Shortly after he recognised his assailant in a bar and called the police. They came and arrested the man, who put up a fight. The respondent had sustained a black eye and his assailant, aged 20, pleaded guilty to causing actual bodily harm and received a fine of £100, which the respondent thought was a correct penalty.

Some of the attacks were clearly for the purposes of robbery, after a victim had put himself in a homosexually compromising situation, and might be expected to be afraid to report the crime:

There were two men in a public lavatory in Brighton when the respondent went in 'cruising' for sex. One of them, a young blond, came up to him. Suddenly, the other one, a larger man, came up behind and grabbed him. They overpowered him after a brief struggle. He was not hurt, but gave them money. Afterwards, he followed them in his car to their house and then called the police. They were arrested. The police were 'friendly and helpful' and warned him the case would be 'messy' as the men would say he had solicited them for sex and given them money when they asked for it. The police wanted to know if he still wished to go on with the case, and he said he did. At the trial the robbers made their allegations as anticipated. In summing up the judge said it was the word of two against one, but that it seemed unlikely the victim would have given chase if he had given them the money, as they said, to keep them quiet. The jury found the men guilty and they were sentenced to three years imprisonment.

BLACKMAIL

Asked about blackmail, 15 of the interviewed men (including five of the 30 'offenders') reported having an experience of that kind; five arose from male love affairs, and seven in the context of casual homosexual encounters with strangers or near strangers. Only three blackmail attempts were by persons exploiting a homosexual man's vulnerability other than in a sexual situation. One of these was by a hitch hiker, to whom no overt approach had been made. He asked the driver if he was gay, and being told 'yes' proceeded to demand money if he were not to complain of sexual assault. He was given £15 to keep him quiet. The second example was a threat against a man working in a hostel for homeless youngsters, by boys he had occasion to reprimand, who retaliated with hints of complaints of impropriety. As he was very open about his homosexuality, which was known to the management as well as the occupants of the hostel, he was not intimidated and the threats were not followed up. The third case was moral blackmail by parents who refused to have contact with their homosexual son or to give him house room unless he became celibate.

With one exception the blackmail attempts by strangers were for money. Several were half hearted and were ignored without anything happening. One man said, 'I just laughed it off'. Another had picked up a young man in his early twenties who threatened to tell the police. He responded by saying he would tell the police himself. Neither of them did so.

None of the victims parted with large sums. One victim was called on by a young man he had picked up and taken home a few days earlier. He was told it would be to his disadvantage if he didn't pay something. He gave £10 with the comment that it would be he who would go to the police next time. He heard no more. In another case, a man of 43 said he had been 'enticed' into a lavatory cubicle by a young man. Once inside his arms were pinioned, some documents forcibly lifted from his pocket, and he was threatened that his employer, whose name was on the stolen papers, would be told if he did not pay up. He was able to get away without paying, having left his wallet in his car. The blackmailer did attempt to contact his employer, but the call was intercepted by a telephonist.

Only two cases resulted in complaints to the police. In one case, a man who had been taken home for sex on several occasions pressed for and was reluctantly given a supposed loan. He then proceeded to commit some blatant thefts. Fearing this was a prelude to serious blackmail the victim went to the police. The victim learned later that a friend had been blackmailed by the same man. The reaction of the police was not described. The other case in which the police were involved arose out of an emotional affair in which a young man became increasingly demanding, wanting money as well as free drinks, and finally, after receiving some £300 over several months, resorting to blows to extort more. At that point the victim went to the police. He freely admitted he was a homosexual. The police were sympathetic. The extortionist was charged and received a suspended sentence of imprisonment. The victim was much embarrassed at the exposure in court of his compromisingly affectionate letters to the young man.

One man had been subjected to blackmail threats when he was only 16, by a middle aged man, the uncle of a school friend. He had allowed himself to be picked up by this man and they had had sex. When they met again, outdoors, he had only wanted to talk, but the older man became angry and tried to force him to allow anal intercourse. He broke free, but the man called out, 'You had better come back or all your friends will get to know about you'. Although very scared by this threat, he ran away and the threat was not carried out.

In two other cases of blackmail by lovers the motive was jealousy or possessiveness, not financial gain. One young man had a lover who was discontented with occasional meetings and wanted to come to live with him. Because he refused the lover carried out a threat to inform his mother, who got into 'a terrible tearful state'. Another man's 'friend' threatened to tell his employer he was a 'poof', unless he gave up seeing a girlfriend. Instead he gave up seeing the man friend. One man was exposed to moral blackmail because his lover, a young man of 19, with a close attachment to his mother, had confided in her. She responded by threatening to inform the police if he saw her son again. They continued to meet clandestinely.

MISCELLANEOUS PROBLEMS

Many of the respondents reported difficulties that would not have arisen but for their homosexuality. Interference with work careers was a particularly common complaint. Asked if they had ever been dismissed or denied promotion on account of their homosexuality, 27 said 'yes' and a further nine said they suspected so. Some of the incidents reported were clear cut examples of intolerance of known homosexual employees, as in the case of the men who had to leave the armed forces; other situations were more ambiguous:

At age 37, when an officer in the Royal Navy, this man started an affair with a seaman on his ship who was aged only 20. They were both in love and it must have been noticeable. A trap was set and they were caught together in his quarters having sex. The officer on duty should have put him under arrest, but did not. The respondent then went ashore and attempted suicide with alcohol and aspirin. He was seen by a naval doctor, transferred to a psychiatric ward and given a medical discharge. He was not allowed to see his seaman friend again and did not know what had happened to him. Although he had escaped trial and publicity, the aftermath left him depressed, drinking to excess, moving from job to job and needing psychiatric treatment after another serious suicide attempt.

He was working as a probationary teacher in a boys' school and had been proposed for a job in a school for the mentally handicapped. When he let slip that he was gay the job never materialised, and from then on attitudes towards him seemed to change. Eventually he was told he had not passed, but he suspects strongly it was because he was gay he was not allowed to proceed.

During ten years in the civil service he told his supervisors, but only some of them were accepting. During a private conversation a personnel officer explained to him that being gay was a reason for not being promoted. All security papers were taken off him and he was never called to promotion boards.

He was working as a ship's steward when he was seen by one of the ship's officers kissing another crew member goodnight after returning from an evening's drinking. He was threatened with dismissal, but transferred to another ship instead.

Respondent said he moved to another branch of medicine (from obstetrics) because it was made clear to him that as a gay man he would not get promotion.

Of course many of those questioned maintained that their work positions had been unaffected or even enhanced by being gay, depending, of course, on the nature of their work and the attitude of superiors:

The respondent, who was a youth worker, said that his boss was also gay and that he had just been promoted in spite of being known at work for being active in the gay movement.

A conviction for importuning at a public lavatory caused everyone at his work to know about his homosexuality, but there were no pressures on him to resign and soon after he was promoted.

Since being openly and publicly involved in a gay organis- ation he has been promoted into work that he would have con- sidered more sensitive than before, because it involves more contact with members of the public.

A question about legal problems other than actual prosecu- tions elicited a curious mixture of experiences. Three men mentioned difficulties in obtaining visas for going abroad, due to a prior conviction. Two men described problems over the receipt of an inheritance. In one case the mother of the respondent's deceased lover threatened to contest the will that had been made in his favour, saying that he had ruined her son, but she did not pursue the case. In another instance a respondent said he was only 16 years old when a lover left him some silver in a will. He did not push to get it because the lover's family were angry.

One respondent, born abroad but allowed to remain in the UK during his current employment, said he was hesitant to apply for permanent residence because of being homosexual. Another had been worried by veiled warnings which he did not under- stand from a social security official who visited his lodgings and questioned him about his gay life.

Another man mentioned that he and his lover tried to obtain a joint mortgage but were refused because they were not a married couple.

One man, who had been separated from an Asian lover when an

immigration officer refused permission for the man to re-enter the country, had pursued a long and unsuccessful legal campaign of appeals, including interventions by an M.P., to try to have the decision reversed. As the large dossier on the matter which the respondent produced showed, he had made clear in his numerous representations that the man was his lover, and regarded as one of his family, but the answers he received made equally clear that homosexual cohabitation was not a relevant consideration in assessing an immigrant's right to remain in the country.

The dissatisfaction of some respondents with the police response to complaints of assault has already been mentioned. Complaints of robbery may also lead to difficulties if the offender makes counter accusations of sexual molestation:

This respondent had his pocket picked and £90 stolen while he was urinating in a public lavatory. He had noticed a black man, whom he took to be gay, hanging about the place, but he had made no approach to him. He reported the incident to the police. Two weeks later he noticed the same man lingering around a different lavatory. He 'phoned the police and they arrived and arrested the offender. At the trial the man concocted an untrue story to the effect that the respondent had been having sex with another person in the toilet and had then approached him and he had been disgusted. To the respondent's great annoyance the man was found not guilty.

Another rather similar story was told by a respondent who said he had been stopped at knife point and forced to take the man to his flat where he was tied up and robbed. He reported the incident to the police who were very cooperative and arrested the man when he contacted the respondent again. At court the man was found not guilty because it was assumed the victim had picked him up.

One respondent said he had once been ordered to leave his lodgings within the week because he had been caught bringing a male friend home for the night. The next example is of a similar incident with less justification:

He used to visit a heterosexual research worker colleague at his lodgings to talk shop. On one occasion they turned off the light to test some apparatus and he heard the landlady's daughter whispering, 'They've turned off the light'. After that his friend was asked to leave. The friend didn't tell him so, but he was sure the landlady had turned his friend out because she thought they were having sex, which was not so.

130

THE 'OFFENDERS'

The 30 offenders reported having been arrested or charged for an offence connected with homosexuality on a total of 46 occasions, 23 for gross indecency, 12 for importuning, one for buggery and ten for a variety of offences. This last group was made up of bye law indecency (one), drunkenness (two), obscene material through the mail (one), obstruction of the police (three), breach of the peace for masturbating in a public lavatory (one) and assaults on police (two). All of these ten arrests were in situations related to homosexuality, such as loitering outside gay bars, participating in gay protests or, in one case, attempting to make an escape from plain clothes officers in the vicinity of a lavatory.

Among these 46 incidents there was one arrest for gross indecency as a juvenile, which did not lead to a charge, and one charge of importuning, which did not result in a conviction because the offender failed to appear at court and apparently no further action was taken.

The experience of being charged was commoner among the least educated 'O' level group (42.5 per cent) than in the remainder of the interviewed sample (25.9 per cent), and this in spite of the least educated being on average three years younger than the others and therefore having had slightly fewer years of risk of arrest; but with such small numbers the trend did not attain statistical significance (10/23 v. 20/77; χ^2 = 2.6, p = 0.11).

One man had been convicted for buggery with boys. He had been accompanied by some under age youths in a public bar. One of the customers objected to their presence and called the police, who began the questioning which led to his imprisonment. Another man had been fined for sending through the post drawings of nude males, which he was selling to a contact magazine. Three men had been convicted for alleged drunkenness, obstruction or assault on police as a result of participating in gay protest demonstrations or congregating in the street outside gay bars. With these few exceptions, all of the offences were related to sexual behaviour in public places. A few of these incidents took place at or near outdoor picking up places, but the majority were in public lavatories. Most of the men had been caught by police in plain clothes who were either watching the lavatory from a hiding place, or lingering at the urinals waiting for some compromising gesture or act.

A quarter of the cases brought to court failed to result in a conviction. Some of the men involved admitted, when

131

interviewed, that they had in fact not been entirely innocent. For example, one man, aged 56 at the time, had been 'cruising' in a public lavatory. He had stood some time at a urinal, looking at other men in the place, and then gone into a cubicle and closed the door, admittedly hoping some 'action' might begin. Instead one of the men from the urinals, who turned out to be a plain clothes police officer, hammered on the door and placed him under arrest. He was put into a police car, together with another man arrested in the same lavatory, taken in for questioning, and charged with importuning. He was a professional man who was able to secure the services of a solicitor known to be sympathetic and efficient. He was acquitted in spite of the police presenting false evidence that he had been seen actually masturbating. The police notified his employer of the nature of the charge against him, but he was not dismissed.

This example was typical of many instances in which offenders admitted that they had been to blame to some extent, but complained of serious misrepresentations or exaggerations in the statements produced by the police.

One convicted man claimed that two men who had been masturbating themselves at urinals beside him proceeded to arrest him as soon as he began to do the same. Another said he had had a pornographic magazine with him when he went into a lavatory and saw a man masturbating at a urinal. He opened the magazine and said to the man: 'This one is good looking'. The man ejaculated, then grabbed him and, together with another officer who suddenly appeared on the scene, arrested him for importuning. These men were bitter about their alleged entrapment, but such cases were exceptional. Most of the informants were clear that provocative behaviour by plain clothes police was limited to the adoption of the dress and demeanour of someone looking for a sexual contact or 'using their youth as a bait', as one man put it.

Most of the prosecuted men admitted that they had been clearly caught out in guilty behaviour. For example, one said that he had been touching 'a nice young man' next to him at a urinal when two young police officers dressed in jeans, one of whom, a short time before, had been standing next to him, leapt down the stairs. One of them was shouting: 'I've got the pair of you'. Another man was caught with a companion in a lavatory cubicle by police who were watching through holes bored through from the ladies' facility next door.

Another respondent, who had been arrested and charged with importuning when he was in his early twenties, had been standing around hoping to pick someone up in the Picadilly Underground concourse in London, a place that was notorious for homosexual prostitution (Harris 1973). The experience was particularly unpleasant because the police assumed he was a male prostitute and he was kept in the police cells from Friday evening until Monday morning, when the magistrate dismissed the case as the evidence against him was insufficient.

It might be thought from these descriptions that police are invariably keen to catch anyone seen behaving suspiciously in a lavatory, but that was not so. One informant, who had been surprised in the act, commented that he had visited lavatories hundreds of times before and never been bothered by the police. Another said that he and several other men had been in an underground lavatory in London at four a.m. when the police came down and told everyone to go home. He left, but returned an hour later. The police came in again. One said, 'I thought I told you to go home'. They asked the number of his car, but took no further action save to say, 'Be a good man and go home!'. Another informant reported that he had been one of a group loitering around a lavatory when the police came along and asked their names. They were not arrested, but told not to be found there again. Another was sexually occupied with a man in a car stationed in a park late at night when a policeman arrived and saw them. They were simply told to go away.

More men than had ever been arrested had put themselves at considerable risk. As many as 59 admitted to having frequented lavatories or outdoor picking up places at least once a week over a period of at least a year at some time in their lives. All but three of the 30 offenders belonged to this 'high risk' category, and of the three exceptions two had never been charged with sexual offences in public. Whether or not they were technically not guilty on the occasion of their arrests, virtually all of the men who had been charged with an offence in public had been in the habit, at some period, of behaving in a way that would have risked arrest. Moreover, many men who freely admitted to having visited lavatories, hundreds if not thousands of times for sexual purposes, had never been charged with an offence of that kind. Of the 100 men seen, 20 said they had been questioned by police in or around lavatories without being charged with an offence. One of these, however, was among the offender group because, on another occasion, he had been arrested.

The consequences of a conviction were very varied. The formal sentence was nearly always a fine, usually no more than £50, but one importuning offence and one of gross indecency each led to no more than a conditional discharge. None of the men reported having been put on probation. One man, who claimed to be technically innocent, although he had been convicted three times previously for lavatory offences, escaped conviction when his alert solicitor prevailed upon the prosecutor to withdraw a charge of importuning so long as he agreed to be bound over. His version of what happened was that a man next to him at a urinal stood at an angle of 45° pointing the end of his penis suggestively. Being rather leery he said, 'Do you want something?', and walked out without waiting for an answer. He was arrested by a police officer on leaving. The first man, also a police officer, accused him of having said, 'Do you want to be sucked?'.

Apart from the man whose sexual friendships with a number of youths came to light through police enquiries, only one other offender was sentenced to imprisonment, and that for lavatory incidents in the early 1950's. Having already been convicted and fined for gross indecency after being caught on a common with a youth, he was sentenced to six months imprisonment on another indecency charge a year or so later. He had been surprised with another man in a lavatory cubicle by two policemen concealed in a broom cupboard. Six months after release from prison he was again caught in a lavatory and received another six months imprisonment. On this occasion he had noticed the shadows of two men together in a cubicle next to him. He thought they were masturbating. He pushed a note under the partition asking if they wanted sex. They were police officers.

The psychological trauma, the reactions of relatives and the blighting of careers were often far more hurtful than the relatively trivial punishments pronounced by the courts, but adverse social consequences were sometimes devastating and sometimes altogether absent, depending upon the offender's personal circumstances and whether the case was mentioned in the local press. For example, one man received a conditional discharge at age 27 when he was caught with another man behind a hedge by police who trailed them from a public lavatory. His name appeared in the local newspapers and he was asked to resign from a promising post as an education officer in a political party. His parents reacted unsympathetically, he had difficulty in finding other employment, and he developed a drink problem. Interviewed over 30 years later, he was doing relatively menial kitchen work in a catering organisation and still expressing bitterness about his wasted career.

In another case, a Methodist minister who was caught with another man in a lavatory cubicle was more fortunate, or perhaps

more resilient. Although his trial got into the national newspapers, as a result, he said, of advance information leaked by
the police, and although one newspaper demanded his dismissal,
he was allowed to continue in his job. His relatives also
proved supportive, but some members of his congregation were
distinctly hostile and he received a spate of unpleasant
letters from strangers.

Following his conviction for importuning in a lavatory when
he was 18, and the appearance of his name and address in a
newspaper, one respondent said he was insulted in the street
and had pornographic material pushed through his letter box.
The resulting strain, and the fear of further harassment, con-
tributed to the ending of the relationship with his lover.

In contrast to these cases there were others for whom a conviction had no effect. One man said he pleaded guilty and was
fined £30. There were no names in the paper and it had no effect on his job. (He thought it had been more upsetting for
the man charged with him). The experience had not stopped him
visiting the same lavatory subsequently. Another offender,
the one prosecuted under a bye law for indecency in a railway
lavatory had a different reaction. He had been allowed to
plead guilty by post without an actual appearance and with no
publicity. He was unemployed at the time, but the police had
told him that they would otherwise have informed his employer.
As he was now working in a youth centre, and would not want to
lose his job, he had given up visiting lavatories.

A third of the cases that came to the courts were said to
have been cited in the press. This was a higher proportion
than the one in seven estimate obtained from a survey of press
cuttings of homosexual cases in 1980 (Meldrum and West 1983).
However, many of the incidents recalled in the present sample
had occurred in much earlier years when newspaper reporting of
such matters may have been more common.

It was clear that lavatory activities were much the most
common cause of prosecution, and it was curious that so many
of the interviewed men admitted to having put themselves at
risk in this way many times. Of course some denied doing so.
In fact 27 said they had never sought sex in lavatories or
outdoor 'cruising' areas. Others claimed to have given up or
greatly reduced such habits, giving as reasons the development
of social contacts or the acquisition of a lover. Some simply
said they had never been drawn to lavatories, because they
were smelly and unattractive, they were risky, or they were
unnecessary in view of the availability of contacts elsewhere.

No one mentioned risk as a reason for the attraction to lavatories. Easy availability was much the commonest explanation.
Men who had spent their youth in small towns or villages where
there was no overt 'gay scene' explained that there was 'no-
where else to go' to find sexual partners. Several recalled
that, when they were young adolescents with strong urges, it
was through calling in lavatories that they first discovered
the possibility of finding other males interested in sex.
Others explained that when young and living with parents, se-
cretive visits to lavatories were easier to engineer and less
likely to attract unfavourable notice than mixing in openly
gay groups. However, many men who had found other outlets
still reverted to lavatory visiting on occasion, in some cases
more particularly at times of loneliness or frustration.

Of the 48 respondents who mentioned 'cottaging' as one of
their first activities in the gay world, 28 had begun by the
age of 18, including eight who had begun by 14. The majority
of this group, 25 out of 28, said they had initially visited
lavatories at least weekly, and 12 of this 25 were still doing
so, although not all of them as frequently as before.

Visiting lavatories was a pursuit that decreased with age:
of 39 respondents who admitted 'cottaging' at least once a
week when they first started going to gay places, 17 said they
had ceased completely, six said they now went to lavatories
only occasionally, and only 16 were still doing so as often as
once a week or more. Of the 30 men who had been habitual 'cot-
tagers' initially (more than once a week) only eight were
continuing at that rate at the time of the interview.

Against this, 11 of the 52 respondents who said that they
did not visit public lavatories when they first started going
to gay places admitted that now they did so, but none of them
as often as once a week. It seemed that, given other alterna-
tives, relatively few men had taken to public lavatories later
in life, and that the preponderance of men who were currently
going to lavatories, and in fact all of those who were still
doing so frequently, had discovered this outlet at an early
stage of their explorations of the gay world.

The 30 'offenders' who were interviewed admitted a total of
23 occasions when they were charged with gross indecency with
youths or men but only one occasion when the charges concerned
involvement with boys under 16. In criminal statistics offences of indecent assault on boys, although rather less common than gross indecency between males, are nothing like so
rare. (In 1982, in England and Wales, 248 men were cautioned
or found guilty of buggery and 725 of indecent assault on a

136

male - both of these being offences nearly always involving boys under 16; whereas 1,237 were cautioned or found guilty of indecency between males and 801 of male soliciting - both being offences rarely involving boys under 16).

Most of the interviewed men denied that they had ever had sex with boys under 16 since they themselves had reached 21, and none mentioned this as a preferred activity. However, eight men recalled having sex with a boy just once and a further 14 reported having done so more often, usually with the same boy or boys on different occasions. Hardly any admitted to prolonged attachments to boys. One man admitted to having sex over a period of months with a boy of 14 who was the son of his living-in housekeeper. The affair came to an end when they moved out. The one respondent who had been imprisoned for offences involving youngsters said that he had contacts with boys under 16 only occasionally, but that with a particular boy he had had a weekly session over a whole year.

Admissions of sexual promiscuity with boys were completely absent, save for one man who said that he had had sex with boys about 20 times in his life. He was apparently a generally promiscuous individual who had been questioned by the police on three different occasions in the vicinity of public lavatories, although he had never been charged.

Several of the respondents who admitted isolated contacts with boys said that they had not known or had mistaken the age of the boy:

> It happened only once. I realised only when he told me he was 14. I thought he was 18. He made the initiative at a holiday camp where I was working.

Another man who had had contact with a 15 year old on two occasions commented, 'He begged me'. Interestingly, one of the men who had reported many contacts when he himself was a boy denied any contacts with boys since he had become adult and said,

> I would never touch a kid who was as young as I was when I started.

The relative rarity of sex contacts with boys among the present sample could be due to under-reporting as a result of reluctance to admit disapproved activities or to acknowledge the true age of younger sex partners. One man commented, 'Often one does not ask their age'. Another said,

> One doesn't know. I'm not attracted to obvious youngsters, but it certainly may have happened.

137

The absence of prosecutions for this behaviour, if not due to untruthfulness - which seems unlikely as respondents were so forthcoming on other topics - suggests that habitual paedophiles, who are most at risk of prosecution for indecency with boys, were omitted from the sample. Perhaps such men do not mix readily among the homosexual groups from which our respondents were mostly drawn, or perhaps if they do they may be reluctant to volunteer to complete questionnaires such as our own.

THE EXPERIENCE OF ARREST

Many of the offenders frankly admitted their guilt and had no real grounds for complaining about their arrest. Some of them spoke in neutral or favourable terms about the attitude of the police. One described them as 'business-like'. Another, caught having sex with a man in a park, was pleased to plead guilty because the police agreed to charge him with the lesser offence of importuning and to keep the matter out of the papers - which they did. On the other hand, perhaps understandably, 21 of the 30 'offenders' were critical of the tactics and attitude of the police during arrest and questioning, complaining of verbal abuse, bullying, intimidation and so forth. Some of those who claimed to have been falsely accused were particularly scathing in their comments, as in the following example.

This man said he used to visit lavatories many times in the past for sexual purposes, but had given up the habit. On the occasion in question he had stopped his car to call at a downstairs facility he knew had a bad reputation, but only because he was genuinely suffering from diarrhoea. All the cubicles were full, but one man was at a urinal and looking around him as if wanting to make contact. After a wait of about half a minute he heard two men coming down the stairs. One said: 'When you hear a scream you'll know what has happened'. Thinking the place might be under attack by 'queer bashers', he left quickly and started up his car. He was obliged to pause at traffic lights, and as he did so two men came up to his car window, one of them shouting to him to open it or he would break it with a stick. 'They looked and behaved like louts', and he drove off not realising that they were policemen, until he was flagged down by a police car and saw the same two men again.

He was taken to a police station, told he was 'in big trouble', accused of trying to run down a policeman, and of having been in the lavatory for 20 minutes for purposes of

138

importuning. It was implied that if only he would admit to the homosexual charge the rest might be forgotten. Shoved around and subjected to lies and bullying, with other officers passing in and out and taking no notice of how he was being treated, he said he quickly lost the good opinion he had always had of the police and he now disliked and feared them. He was charged. He claimed that the evidence given by the police at the Crown Court was blatantly untrue, but his counsel was able to expose its inconsistencies and he was acquitted.

Other complaints about the police included frighteningly aggressive demeanour, derisory comments, pressure to plead guilty and, above all, unnecessary approaches to employers or relatives, with sometimes serious consequences. For instance, one man had been caught in indecent acts with someone sitting next to him in a London cinema - a place no longer in existence but once notorious for homosexual encounters. The police went to the company where he was working in a distant town and told them about the charge. He felt obliged to resign, to his employers' evident relief. Another offender, who had been discovered with a group of men in a lavatory that was suddenly raided by two policemen with an alsation dog, was detained several hours, strip searched, subjected to very hostile questioning, and told that his employers would be notified. He finally came out, as he said, 'almost suicidal', to appear at court next morning and plead guilty, the police having told him 'that would be best'. He was fined £20.

Another man, arrested in a lavatory and found guilty of indecency said the police lied in court, claiming he had been engaged in flagrant masturbation. He claimed that the arresting officer harassed him verbally afterwards, saying, 'If we're out to get you we'll get you'. As long as three years later the same arresting officer shouted out 'fairy' to him in the street. Yet another respondent, a clergyman, who had been arrested for sexual misconduct in a lavatory cubicle, recalled that the police had been hostile and abusive and insisted on using handcuffs, although he was perfectly willing to go with them. A nursing tutor, arrested as he was leaving a lavatory, described a similar scene: handcuffed, verbally abused ('dirty fuckers' etc.), kept five hours in the police station and subjected to great pressure to make a statement and plead guilty. Another man, arrested in a lavatory by policemen who emerged from a cleaner's cupboard, said he was marched with hands behind his back down the main street of the town, made to stand in a corner for an hour, thrown across and pushed around a police cell and threatened that his employers would be told. After ten hours, he finally agreed at one a.m., to sign a statement that the police had prepared for him saying he had been masturbating with another man, when in reality they had been interrupted before that stage was reached.

Among those who claimed to have been innocent of the charge against them was one man who said he had been waiting for a friend for 30 minutes in a West End street, near where he had a shop. Seeing someone he thought he knew he went up to him and said a tentative 'hello', followed by a few sentences like 'Where have you been?'. The man turned out to be a plain clothes policeman, and a second policeman suddenly appeared and he was arrested for importuning. The area was one known for homosexual prostitution. He pleaded not guilty and the case went to a jury trial. The six months of waiting was a horrible period in his life. He felt dirty and angry because the police had lied, saying they saw him trying to pick up three different men. The jury was out five hours, coming back twice before finally reaching a majority verdict of guilty. He lost self confidence and felt ill and unhappy afterwards.

In another instance, an interviewee who had been arrested for gross indecency said that he had merely been urinating behind a bill board. There were other men there who made off when the police arrived. He claimed that the police were aggressive and bullying, as if he had committed some moral outrage against them. He was acquitted.

In only one case was it alleged that the police had hinted that a bribe might avoid an arrest. This was a man who had been with an airman behind a hedge, when accosted by two policemen. The airman ran off chased by one of the officers. The remaining officer got into conversation with him about his work and remarked, 'You've made a botch up', and later, 'Make it worth my while and perhaps I can do something about it'. He thought the policeman meant that he would be allowed to run away as well, but he did not accept because he felt he had not been in the wrong, since he had not actually touched the airman. He said he would go to the police station. He was in fact convicted, having been advised to plead guilty to avoid publicity.

It was not only the police that some offenders claimed had treated them badly. One man said he had been just talking with his friend when a policeman came into a urinal and shone a torch. Because he had an erection, which always happened to him in these places, they were both arrested for gross indecency. The policeman was said to have been 'kind and pleasant', but his solicitor said he wouldn't represent him unless he pleaded guilty, because the case was 'so disgusting', and also

140

because he had 'no defence', since he had admitted to homosexual behaviour on other occasions. (This was before the
1967 Act which decriminalised private homosexual behaviour).
He was fined and his friend, who had a previous conviction,
was imprisoned. He felt guilty and confided in an RAF padre,
who reported to an RAF doctor, who put him into a psychiatric
hospital and prescribed castration. On learning of his conviction his father disinherited him and had hardly any contact
with him again. He was also refused employment in a shipping
company on account of this conviction, and he could not emi-
grate to America, as he wanted, because he knew he would be
refused a visa.

Another respondent, who had been caught embracing a man in
the dark in a public park, was accused by the police of having
been engaged in fellatio. He said his solicitor 'didn't help
at all'. She treated him like dirt and commented, 'sucking
cocks in parks is what all gay men do'.

Although none of the offenders could have found being arrested or charged a pleasant experience, a few of them did des-
cribe the attitude of the police in quite favourable terms:

They were really more decent than might have been expected.

They were quite professional - business-like.

[After arrest for lavatory importuning] the police seemed
friendly. Radioed for a car. Kept at the police station
one hour.

CONTRASTS BETWEEN 'OFFENDERS' AND MATCHED 'NON-OFFENDERS'

The group of 30 respondents who admitted having been charged
or arrested for a homosexual offence were matched individually
with 30 who had not and who were of the same educational category and of similar age (i.e. not more than five years difference). As can be seen from Table 12.2 the 'offender' group
included more individuals who had been at 'high risk' of arrest, more who currently went 'cottaging' or 'outdoor cruising'
and more who had been questioned by the police without being
charged. That their behavioural style may have tended to be
more provocative than that of the 'non-offenders' was suggested
by the larger number who had experienced a physical attack on
account of their homosexuality. Of the physical attacks reported by the 'offender' group, a higher proportion took place
at lavatories and cruising areas and fewer were reported by the
victim to the police.

A hint that there might be more social alienation among the

Table 12.2

Items elicited at interviews distinguishing 'offenders' and 'non-offenders' matched for age and educational level

	Group of 30 arrested or charged	Matching group of 30 'non-offenders'
Been at 'high risk' of arrest	26	12
Still go 'outdoor cruising'	16	5
Currently go 'cottaging'	18	9
Currently 'cottage' at least weekly	7	4
Been questioned by police at least once without being charged	15	10
Have no regular lover	21	14
Currently unemployed	6	1
Has been physically attacked	19	10
(Total number of attacks reported by (group (	30	13
(Total attacks at lavatories or cruising (areas (	13	3
(Total attacks reported by victim to (police	7	5
Admitted homosexuality to boss	17 (of 26)	7 (of 24)
Admitted homosexuality to mother	16	15
Admitted homosexuality to father	9	8
Classed among the 37 most 'overt'	12	7

offender group was given by the observation that more of them were currently unemployed and fewer had any regular lover. More of them had been open about their homosexuality to bosses at work, but that could have been because they were not in a position to conceal it. The number who admitted their homosexuality to their parents was about the same in the two groups.

CONTENTMENT AND DISCONTENTMENT

As already noted, and notwithstanding the number of disagreeable experiences resulting from their homosexuality, the vast majority of the interviewed men would not have wanted their orientation altered. Many of them considered that there were advantages as well as disadvantages. All of them were asked, in open ended questions, to say what they felt were the 'good things' and what were the 'bad things' about living as a gay person. They were invited to cite as many items as they wished. Their comments were very varied, but it was possible to assign many of them to one or other of a few common categories, as shown in Table 12.3.

Some respondents felt that there were no intrinsically good or bad things about gay living: eight replied to the former question and nine to the latter with such comments as, 'I don't think there are any' or 'Nothing in particular'. The freedom and personal independence afforded by a gay life style was the most commonly reported advantage, mentioned by 45 respondents in such terms as the following:

The freedom to come and go as you like.

Not being legally tied to anyone.

Independence, freedom to travel.

Freedom from conventional behaviour, more of a choice.

It gives one a wide freedom of choice in relationships.

Options in life are more open out of the straightjacket of a wife and kids and a mortgage.

Freedom to choose your life style.

Independence!

One has only oneself to please.

Perhaps I wouldn't need the freedom of gay life if I were heterosexual, but I have a strong need for not being tied.

We don't have the responsibilities of heterosexuals - practical, financial or emotional. We can please

Table 12.3

Number of citations of various 'good' and 'bad' things
about a gay life style

Good things		Bad things	
Can't think of any	9	Can't think of any	8
Freedom	45	Discrimination	45
Good social life	25	Restriction on social life	9
No family responsibilities	23	No family	15
Good sex life	18	Behaviour in gay scene	20
Financial advantage	12	Enforced reserve	21
Good friendships	17	Loneliness	13
		Work problems	16
		Legal or police discrimination	14

144

ourselves.

In addition to these general comments, 23 respondents mentioned specifically the benefits of freedom from family responsibilities. This mostly referred to not having the
responsibility of bringing up children, although avoidance of
the marriage tie and monogamy was also cited occasionally:

It gets you out of the family situation and family commit-
ments. Not being in a conventional marriage gives you a
freedom which married people don't have.

Being free of the constraints of a legal marriage or the
pressure of having kids and the restriction to one partner.

I'm independent, not trapped into marriage like many
heterosexuals.

It's good not to have children, not to have responsibilities.

Freedom, absence of children.

Much more freedom than my straight friends. I like travel
and being able to go off when I want without worrying
about home and kids.

There were fewer citations, 15 in all, of the disadvantages
of not having a family, and these were mostly in connection
with wanting to have children:

It's bad for those who want children.

I'd have liked to be settled with a wife and able to bring
up children. A platonic marriage is not satisfactory.

No children.

Restricted family, that is not having children.

Denied the comforts and companionship of family life.

Lack of family.

Not having a wife to look after me.

Some respondents saw the lack of children and marriage as
having both good and bad aspects:

It's a balance. The advantages [of freedom] have to be
balanced against not having a wife as a partner for life.
And I should have liked to have kids.

The good social life enjoyed by gay men was mentioned by 25
respondents, who commented on the ease of making contact with
a variety of interesting people:

145

Gay people are more interesting to know.

I've met a lot of lovely people.

A much more active social life.

A type of freemasonry. You can get to know a large number of people more easily.

The "world club", making it easy to meet people and have friendship bonds around the world.

One can spend a night with interesting people just through being gay, with no risks of pregnancy. You can meet people all over the world on that basis. It's wonderful!

The pleasure one gets from being with other gay people. They're more fun.

The best discos and pubs are gay.

I enjoy the social scene.

Lots of different friends from different backgrounds.

The quality of friendships amongst gay people was praised by 17 respondents, as being better than in heterosexual society:

There's a great camaraderie, a sense of community.

The sense of solidarity as an oppressed minority tends to create honesty.

Relationships split up without the hostility and problems that heterosexuals have. Gay love is stronger than love among heterosexuals.

I like gay people.

Gay friends are more sincere.

More love, trust and affection - all much stronger among gays than among straights.

In general, gay people seem more intelligent, more civilised, pleasant and broad-minded than straights.

The rules of relationships are better, more reasonable and honest.

Friendships are very positive. The gay life style puts friendships in a positive focus.

The opportunity for making sexual contacts, or the quality of sex life, which might have been thought to be a prime reason for adopting a specifically gay life style, was mentioned by 18 men:

Frequency of sex. Casual sex if you want.

I lead a very active sex life and have no sex hang-ups
like many heterosexuals. A very free sex life.

In contrast, nine men felt that friendships and social life
were constricted:

Exclusion from the interests and social life of the
majority.

I don't like being part of a little club and the all male-
ness of gay life. I believe in the desegregation of the
sexes.

You're deprived of the experiences of the majority, which
makes it difficult to relate to them.

The favourable comments about the good quality of gay relationships were more than balanced by 20 men who complained of
the behaviour of other gays and of the attitudes prevalent on
the gay scene:

Because of their independence people are a bit casual.
Gay people can be shallow.

Fear of losing one's partner is endemic in the gay world.

Fear of my lover leaving, which happens in the gay world.
Open relationships undermine the basic relationship.

It can get too loose sexually. People can be affected.

It's hard to have a true marriage as a gay person.

There's more bitchiness and backbiting on the gay scene.
People are two-faced or whatever.

There's some bitchiness and some selfishness among gays.
Some try to split people up. Not all gays, only a few are
like that, but they are worse than straights.

There are things I can't talk to a lover about as one
could to a wife. If I'm ill I feel totally alone.

A wild sex life can be negative - disease.

I feel anger and frustration from not being able to share
the good and bad of life with another person.

Self obsession is more among gay people than straights.

There are aspects of the ghetto mentality which I don't
like.

The wish to be promiscuous. The sexual rat race.

The financial advantages of not having to support a family
or being able to share house with another man were mentioned

147

by 12 respondents:

> You should be better off financially with two male wages. You can go out more.

> I enjoy having more money.

> On a material level gays are a lot better off - witness their expenditure in pubs.

By far the most commonly mentioned negative aspect of gay living, cited by 45 respondents, was discrimination or lack of acceptance by heterosexual society. Apart from general comments on this, 16 respondents cited specifically problems related to work and 14 mentioned legal or police discrimination. Only five of these 14, however, were among the 30 men who had actually been charged with a homosexual offence:

> Inevitable guilt feelings because of social unacceptability.

> Having to be concerned about other people's reactions. Always the possibility of being rejected. People not wanting to know you because you are gay.

> A barrier to professional advancement. You have to put up a front in order to move up in a profession.

> Prejudice you continually have to fight.

> Very divisive pressures are put on gays. It has a negative effect on one's self esteem.

> Very much a risk of career damage. Society may pretend [otherwise], but it is not tolerant.

> Scorned by media, socially unacceptable, ridiculed.

> Discrimination by heterosexuals.

> Isolation from work colleagues.

> Always a doubt about a job interview when living with another gay.

> Homosexuality is a minority thing. Society does not cater to singles and gays.

> Not being able to be yourself, your relationship not being seen as valid. Discrimination by people in society - great social pressure.

> Discrimination, and the anger one feels against the self congratulation of the heterosexual world.

Closely related to the topic of discrimination was the need for secrecy, or at least discretion, which was referred to as a negative item by 21 respondents, as in the following examples:

It can be embarrassing. That's why I keep so much to myself.

There's still a kind of prejudice. I don't go around telling people I'm gay.

I'd like to be open and still able to keep friends. It's difficult being open. Supervisors and colleagues at work always assume I'm straight.

Nervousness at being found out or caught in gay activities.

Lack of openness. Makes people devious. Affects character development.

Every day you face decisions whether to come out to a particular person. It's difficult to be casual about it.

Fear of exposure with loss of job or spoiled career because of the bad opinion straights have of gays.

Loneliness was mentioned by only 13 respondents (16.3 per cent of those over 40, 10.5 per cent of those under 40). This does not support the view that loneliness is a major problem at any age, but it may be that our survey failed to reach the more isolated homosexuals.

Among miscellaneous unclassified negative comments, only three respondents mentioned venereal disease, although at the time the interviews were being conducted the epidemic of acquired immune deficiency syndrome (AIDS) was receiving great publicity, especially in the gay press.

Among the miscellaneous unclassified comments, a major theme was that gay living had encouraged questioning of conventional attitudes, independence of mind, self sufficiency, and a sympathetic understanding of personal problems.

Gay people have to think more about their relationships.

It makes you more tolerant of others' differences.

It makes you question what life is all about.

Gays are not so tied to conformity. Can keep a weather eye on events. More time and commitment to causes.

More potential for personal growth - opening of oneself up to many experiences, expanding awareness on all levels of life. Not tied down by creed or dogma.

It gives you greater sensitivity and understanding of other people and society and makes you less prone to prejudiced judgements about others.

NOTES

[1] Where the first person singular is used in the quotations this indicates an approximation to the respondent's actual phrases; where the third person is used it represents the interviewer's summary of what was said.

13 Conclusions

Generalisations from the results of this survey can be made
only very cautiously and tentatively in view of the nature of
the sample. No apology need be made for these limitations,
since it is quite impracticable to obtain a completely representative, unbiassed selection of 'homosexuals'. In the first
place the very definition of a homosexual is uncertain. For
example, it is open to question whether to exclude or include
in a study of homosexuality family men leading an ostensibly
heterosexual life style with only occasional incursions into
the gay scene, ambisexuals who are equally at home with a
partner of either gender, those who have pronounced homosexual
yearnings that they have never put into practice, or persons
who experience alternating periods of heterosexual and
homosexual preference.

The present survey was almost entirely restricted to men who
had developed, sometimes at a very early age, sometimes after
a previous heterosexual phase, a strong and apparently permanent same sex preference, and who identified themselves as
gay or homosexual, and who had for the most part established
links with a circle of gay friends or with an overt gay community. Had this not been the case, they would have been unlikely to have heard about and received the questionnaire that
brought them into the study. Furthermore, the sample necessarily included only those willing to fill in a questionnaire
and the interviewed subsample consisted of those willing to

pear in person and discuss their personal lives with a researcher. Although many of those who received the questionnaires filled them in, and most of those who did so agreed to
an interview, one cannot know whether certain categories of
person excluded themselves from the investigation. It might
be that individuals with experiences of which they were
ashamed, such as those with a predilection for contacts with
children or individuals anxious to conceal their homosexual
orientation, would be less likely to come forward.

Only rarely was there any clue as to reasons for non-
response. One man who declined to fill in a questionnaire
when asked in person said that he was working in a sensitive
job (actually in social work) and as a matter of principle
would not wish to become involved. Another man, who initially
agreed to an interview, but then failed to turn up or to
answer follow up letters, had become engaged to a girl, and
although still active homosexually, may have wished to dis-
tance himself from his previous contacts with gay organisations. (This information came from one of those who was
interviewed who happened to know him well).

Because of the way the questionnaires were initially distributed, the sample was over-weighted with well educated men in
white collar occupations, and also with individuals actively
interested in gay rights or gay politics. Consequently, many
were forthright and expressive, as well as intellectually ana-
lytical about their place in society and the wider implications of a homosexual orientation. This was helpful in
providing revealing descriptions, but was probably not typical
of ordinary, non-intellectual homosexuals, who were under-
represented among our interviewees.

The findings therefore raise issues that cannot be settled
without further research. For example, the fact that relatively few of the interviewed men were in superior professional
or managerial occupations consistent with their advanced education might be explained in various ways. Such persons may
have felt too busy to give time to filling in a questionnaire
or reluctant to risk compromising their position in any way.
Alternatively, it could be that homosexual interests run
counter to professional advancement (as some respondents suggested from their own experience), and that some men who
would otherwise have occupied higher positions settled for or
were relegated to less responsible positions with less public
exposure.

Homosexual activities with teenagers were mentioned quite
freely by some of the interviewed men, but not activities with

152

young children, even though recollections of having contacts with older men when they themselves were children were quite commonly reported. Since only one man out of the 443 questionnaire respondents admitted a conviction for sex with a boy (with one prosecuted but not convicted and one other questioned but not charged), it is highly likely that paedophiles either declined to respond or were largely absent from the groups who received the questionnaire. Consequently, our study reveals hardly anything about involvement in the more serious types of homosexual offence. The findings do lend some support, however, to the belief that sexual interest centred upon young children is not a phenomenon commonly observed among males who socialise in adult gay circles, and therefore, for them, not a common cause of confrontation with the law. Those who did describe behaviour with youths that could have rendered them liable to prosecution referred to consensual activities with sexually mature partners who were near to or above what would be the age of consent for a girl.

It has already been mentioned that a survey similar to our own was conducted in England some 25 years ago by the sociologist Michael Schofield, writing under the name of Westwood (1960). He obtained, in much the same way as ourselves, a roughly comparable sample of predominantly middle class, self defined homosexual males. Similar to the results from our own study, Westwood found that only two per cent of his interviewed men had been convicted for offences with minors. Among our interviewees, 14 per cent reported having had sexual contacts more than once with a boy under 16 since they were 21. Westwood found that 12 per cent of his sample had engaged in homosexual activities with boys of 16 or under since they were 18. We identified no true paedophiles among the interviewed men, although one or perhaps two had a preference for young adolescents. Westwood found two paedophiles who were exclusively interested in sex with boys under 16. He concluded, as we did, that true paedophiles were comparatively rare among respondents drawn from the friendship circles of ordinary gay men.

Information about persistent child molesters is unlikely to be obtained from this type of study. Such persons are more frequent among clients of the criminal courts, probably because they have put themselves at greater risk of prosecution. Westwood noted, as we did, that the minority of respondents who admitted having had some contacts with boys nearly all described these as no more than occasional events, usually opportunistic, and not necessarily preferred to contacts with more mature males. He also noted that in 15 per cent of his respondents their first recalled homosexual contact took place with an adult and before they had reached the age of 17. We did not ask this question, although we did note that many respondents mentioned contacts in public lavatories, presumably with adults, when they were boys.

These findings suggest that contacts between boys and adult males are not uncommon; they often occur because the boy wants the contact and deliberately sets out to make himself available. Given the opportunity some homosexual men will have contacts with boys, although this is not a preferred or exlusive sexual practice among the vast majority. In this respect the homosexual population is probably not substantially different in behaviour and inclination from the heterosexual male's outlook towards young girls. It is possible that homosexual men who occasionally indulge in contacts with adolescent boys put themselves at greater risk of arrest than do heterosexuals behaving similarly with adolescent girls.

The prime purpose of the survey was to assess the nature and extent of the social and legal problems encountered as a result of having a homosexual orientation. Since the number of persons questioned by the police in connection with homosexuality or charged with a homosexual offence was proportionately greater among the less well educated, and since the sample was evidently biassed towards persons favoured by superior education and having supportive contacts with the gay community, it can be fairly safely assumed that our statistics of reported problems would tend to under-estimate rather than to exaggerate the incidence of problems experienced by homosexual males in general. Even so, the incidences in this sample of certain specific adverse experiences, such as police questioning, physical assault, and rejection by friends, relatives or co-workers, were surprisingly high.

On the other hand, many respondents had little or nothing to report by way of adverse experiences, and many of the interviewed men appeared contented, problem free and surprised that they had been selected for an interview because they had so little to report. As one affluent company director, whose only significant adverse experience was that he had once had his wallet stolen by a pick-up who 'turned nasty', explained,

> I have been fortunate to own my own house in the country and flat in London and also fortunate in never suffering any harassment from neighbours.

It did appear that the socially advantaged were less exposed than others to public scrutiny, street attacks, or confrontations with police, perhaps because they had greater opportunity to behave as freely as they wanted in circumstances of privacy without calling attention to themselves.

The questions on which the research was based were deliberately made fairly specific, seeking for accounts of concrete instances of adverse experiences that would serve to indicate the frequency and severity of homosexuals' social problems. A number of respondents, who had no particularly glaring examples to report, made the point that their real problem was not so much open or dramatic acts of hostility as a pervasive sense of oppression and devaluation in the face of the unsympathetic and dismissive attitudes of the heterosexual majority, the derisive comments of authority figures and media, and the suspicion, rather than proof, that being homosexual put them at a subtle disadvantage in such situations as selection for promotion.

There were, however, more than enough examples of overt conflict or confrontation to validate the impression that a male homosexual orientation is still a source of difficulty in Britain. The felt need for concealment, although less prominent among the younger generation, was one of the commonest causes for concern. Many who had been able to be open with their peer group had not felt able to confide in parents, and some of those who had done so had experienced temporary and occasionally permanent rejection. The theoretical tolerance of homosexuality to which intellectual liberals so often subscribe does not always extend to welcoming the phenomenon in one's own son. The number of men who said they had lost friends, particularly male friends, through revealing their homosexuality, was a further indication of the reluctance of many people to become too closely involved with someone openly gay, and would seem to account, at least in part, for the fact that so many respondents said that all their close friends were gay.

The surprisingly high prevalence of histories of physical assault confirms the impression given by examples published by the Campaign for Homosexual Equality (Meldrum 1979). Becoming the victim of an unprovoked assault by a 'queer basher', as described at some of the interviews, could be regarded as proof positive of vulnerability to the extreme hostility of some sections of the public. However, provocation is a question of degree. Many of the attacks were reported to have taken place outside gay bars or in vicinities notorious for homosexual 'cruising', where the victims may have been rather blatantly advertising their unpopular interests. A few of the assaults were the result of lovers' quarrels, or by dissatisfied prostitutes, or by men affronted by a homosexual approach, and in these instances the victim's interaction with the

155

assailant was an important element. Particularly dramatic, however, were those cases in which a casual sexual contact, after some preliminary sexual interchange, or even after apparently very satisfactory completion of love-making, suddenly became violent. The self hatred, and hatred of others similarly inclined, which afflicts some homosexuals and causes irrational upsurges of rage in sexual situations, can be extremely dangerous and adds to the various risks which homosexuals who like promiscuous sex with strangers are prone. 'Closeted' homosexual males who seek sexual contacts only occasionally, and who lack the experience and sophistication in handling such situations that was displayed by many in our sample, probably incur even greater risks (Miller and Humphreys 1980).

The interactions between homosexuals and police, a topic of some interest and current controversy, proved, according to our respondents, to be more varied than expected. There were quite enough instances alleged of bullying, unnecessary hostility, questionable techniques of entrapment, false or exaggerated evidence in court, and crimes disregarded because the complainant was homosexual, to support the popular notion that the police are prejudiced and antagonistic towards homosexual men. On the other hand there were many instances described in which the police had acted kindly, helpfully or with discretion. The number of occasions when men were charged with importuning or indecency in public were fewer than the occasions on which men had been questioned or warned about such behaviour without any further police action being taken. Some of the victims of robbery, assault and blackmail who went to the police were treated with consideration and the offenders charged. Even among the respondents who had actually been arrested, some described the behaviour of the police in such terms as 'reasonable' or 'business-like'.

Expressions of suspicion of, or even antagonism towards, authority were expressed by some of the interviewed men, but attitudes to the police were by no means uniformly negative. The fact that descriptions of police behaviour were so varied suggests that what happens in the course of these confrontations very much depends on the individual officers involved and the policy in operation at any particular time and in any particular locality. Some of the accounts of misbehaviour by the police, if they are accurate, do point to the need for stricter control and more enlightened approaches. The reluctance of homosexual victims to report incidents to the police, which came out clearly in their accounts, is a direct and unfortunate consequence of their not entirely unjustified anticipation of being treated unsympathetically.

156

Comparison between our own findings and those of Westwood, 25 years ago, provide some tentative indication of the consequences of the social changes that have occurred in the intervening decades, including the decriminalisation of consensual homosexual contacts between adult males that took place with the passing of the Sexual Offences Act 1967. Westwood reported that ten per cent of his sample had been assaulted at some time. These assaults generally were made by casual sexual partners - often in the course of robbery, but sometimes 'in the deflationary period that follows orgasm' apparently as 'atonement for strong guilt feelings'. According to our questionnaire respondents, nearly 30 per cent had been physically attacked because of their homosexuality, but of those who had been attacked only 15 per cent said their assailants were casual sex partners. Most of the attacks were said to be by a group of strangers, and the follow up interviews showed that this usually meant attacks in public places such as the street (23 out of the 73 reported attacks having taken place in the vicinity of lavatories or 'cruising' areas). Westwood does not mention assaults of this 'queer bashing' kind, which probably means that they were less frequent when his enquiry was carried out. If there has been a significant increase in these incidents, it could be the result of increasing awareness of homosexuality by the public at large, and the consequential ease with which hostile youths are nowadays able to identify members of the gay fraternity. It remains true that only a minority of assaulted men make a complaint to the police; one in six in Westwood's sample, one in four in our sample.

Blackmail seems to have been a more serious problem for homosexuals in the 1950's. Westwood recorded that 13 per cent of his sample had been subjected to blackmail threats for money, and a half of those threatened had paid up, sometimes repeatedly over a considerable period of time. Among our questionnaire respondents only 10.5 per cent reported any kind of blackmail. In the follow up interviews it turned out that a considerable minority of blackmail incidents (six out of 15) were not concerned with extorting money, and of the financial blackmail incidents the attempts were largely opportunistic and involved only single payments of quite small sums. Most of the interviewed men who had been blackmailed did not seem to have treated it as a major concern.

This apparent reduction in the seriousness of blackmail threats probably reflects a greater openness about homosexuality today which, as already noted, is especially evident among the younger generation. Westwood did not ask specific questions about openness. He was working at a time when homosexual behaviour was still criminal, when discretion was the accepted norm, and before the 'gay liberation' movement in the 1970's made 'coming out' a feasible choice for gay men. Even so, he noted that nearly a fifth of his sample were to some extent open about their sexual preferences at their place of work. About a half of the men we interviewed reported some degree of frankness with their colleagues at work, which certainly points to a lessening of secrecy. It was noticeable, however, that this increased openness had not always led to satisfactory integration into ordinary society. Many of our respondents referred to 'straights' and the straight life style in terms suggestive of a distinctly alien culture, much as heterosexuals have tended to refer to the homosexual subculture as a group apart from the rest of society. Among the men we interviewed, 81 per cent said that most of their close male friends were also homosexual.

As noted earlier, Westwood's figures for arrests for homosexual offences were essentially similar to our own, except for the eight per cent of his sample who had a conviction for homosexual activities in private with an adult - behaviour which would not be prosecutable among civilians today. The criticisms he recorded of police behaviour in connection with arrests - that is the use of 'agent provocateur' tactics and bullying and threats to secure an admission of guilt - were similar to allegations made by some of our interviewees. However, since Westwood reported only negative comments about the police it is not possible to know how far the treatment of arrested homosexuals has changed. In Westwood's sample it appears that all 25 men charged with a homosexual offence had pleaded guilty and signed incriminating statements. This was apparently quite usual at the time, according to the Wolfenden Report (Home Office 1956, para.142). At the trials of our own interviewed men, nearly a half pleaded not guilty and a quarter were found not guilty. This was a significant change from the custom at the time of Westwood's study, and suggests an increased awareness of civil rights and willingness to contest charges, notwithstanding the risk of unfavourable publicity. Neither Westwood nor ourselves asked specifically about the treatment of those accused of homosexual offences by their lawyers, but in both surveys about a fifth of the interviewed men commented unfavourably, usually suggesting that their defence had been hampered by unsympathetic representation.

Arrest for behaviour in or around public lavatories remains a common risk for many homosexual males, although nowadays a conviction for such behaviour less often results in imprisonment. With the recent proliferation of gay bars and gay organisations one might have expected the need to resort to lavatories to diminish, except perhaps for married men and others in situations that do not permit them to socialise in openly gay places (Humphreys 1979). Our sample did not include such persons, and it was evident that, even among men capable of making sexual contacts in other ways, lavatories still met a felt need at times for easy, quick contacts with no necessary personal commitment. The lavatory habit, when present, had usually developed early in life (perhaps when other opportunities were lacking) and there was some tendency to revert to it as a supplementary outlet or perhaps during periods of loneliness. The likelihood of arrest on any given occasion was too slight to act as an effective deterrent.

Part III

D. J. WEST

14 Lessons to be drawn

One point that stands out from the findings of both these studies is the striking variation in attitudes to sexual matters which exists within our society. We are said to live in an age of sexual permissiveness, but individual opinions as to what sexual behaviours are desirable, permissible, obnoxious or seriously criminal differ remarkably. In spite of the theoretical tolerance towards homosexual behaviour that has become intellectually fashionable, investigation reveals that some degree of condemnation is widespread and emotional abhorrence not uncommon. Good evidence for this was provided by the number of parents who were seriously upset, in some cases to the point of absolute rejection, when they learned of a son's homosexuality, and the relatively few families prepared to accept a man's male lover as they would have accepted a wife or girlfriend. The incidence of gratuitous physical assaults reported by homosexuals, as well as attacks from partners 'turning nasty' after casual sexual indulgence, bear witness to the continuance of strong feelings of disapproval or disgust.

In regard to non-violent sexual contacts between young girls and older males, attitudes are just as varied. It is sometimes argued that many girls are physically mature, and quite capable of deciding what sexual relations they desire, long before the legal 'age of consent'. It is also sometimes argued that younger children have sexual feelings and

163

interests, are far from being the 'little innocents' of Victorian theory, and that many of them solicit and enjoy, and are not in the least damaged by, sexual attentions from adults. Although some of the experiences recounted in our study fitted this image, others were more in keeping with the commoner stance, which views adult child sexual contacts as highly reprehensible, frightening and off-putting to the child, and potentially damaging to future sexual adjustment. Indeed, it appeared that some parents were so horrified at the idea of their own child being contaminated by such contacts that they reacted in ways that caused more trauma than the incident itself, for instance by disbelieving the child's story, being more concerned with apprehending the adult than looking after the child, or even blaming the child for being the instigator.

Both these enquiries suggested that problematic sexual behaviour is often made more problematic by over-reaction on the part of persons in whom strong feelings of disapproval are aroused. Some of the women interviewed in the enquiry into child sexual abuse wanted offenders executed or castrated, yet many of the 'abusive' incidents reported seemed rather trivial (such as confrontations with an exhibitionist) and very few involved serious physical brutality. Although most of the women remembered finding the incidents unpleasant, sometimes extremely unpleasant and frightening, only a minority claimed to have had lasting effects. A desire for capital punishment, therefore, seems disproportionate and indicative of an over-valuation of misbehaviour that has sexual connotations.

This over-valuation can have unfortunate results for the children involved. Interrogations by officials, in efforts to bring perpetrators to justice, can be more distressing than the sexual incidents, as a number of the women explained. Worse still, the removal of a girl from her family and into a children's home, in order to protect her from the risk of further sexual incidents (a move of questionable efficacy if she is placed among a crowd of maladjusted and delinquent young people) can affect her development and social prospects more seriously than the sexual molestation. The one woman in our study who described such a move did so in most unfavourable terms. Mothers who, in ignorance of the likely consequences, have confided to a social worker their worries about the suspicious behaviour of their husband towards a daughter or stepdaughter, all too often find themselves before long struggling to look after the children alone on welfare handouts, while the husband is serving a long term of imprisonment. Then, when the offender is due for release, the wife is forced to choose between having him back with her or having her children taken away by the social services because they are considered to be at continuing risk of molestation.

Some experienced therapists, notably in Holland and in California, where greater discretion is exercised when cases of domestic child sexual abuse are disclosed, find that psychological support and counselling, avoiding police intervention or prosecution, often suffices to bring misconduct to an end. The break up of the whole family, which is the last thing most child victims want to happen, is not usually necessary. In this country, however, some social workers, even though they might be willing to allow a child who has been subjected to physically injurous treatment to remain in the parental home, would not want to take that risk in the mildest case of sexual misconduct. Likewise, some of our prosecuting authorities take the view that, in the interest of the public at large, and to mark society's abhorrence, the break up of a family is a small price to pay for bringing an offender to justice.

Over-reaction is also evident in the matter of homosexual nuisances in public lavatories. Some policemen, it seems, are particularly harsh in their handling of men arrested for these offences, and some are willing (at least unofficially) to use provocative tactics in making arrests that would not be countenanced in relation to more serious crimes. Nevertheless, as the survey showed, there is considerable variation in police behaviour, as there is in the attitudes of the public at large, and detected offenders are quite likely to be given no more than a warning. Furthermore, as in the matter of sexual contacts between adults and children, infinitely more incidents occur than ever come to official notice. This makes it appear that the minority who are prosecuted, and who, in addition to incurring a legal penalty, may suffer greatly from newspaper publicity, are being made scapegoats.

Newspapers have a lot to answer for in this regard. Publishing the names of men guilty of sexual indecencies has the result of breaking up families, ruining careers, and bringing great suffering upon children. Although there are legal safeguards to prevent the name of a child sex victim being published, if the name of the father or stepfather appears in connection with a charge of indecent assault on a girl or boy, that suffices to inform the neighbourhood and cause great embarrassment to, and sometimes ostracism of, the affected children by their peers. Of course, in the last resort it is the public which is to blame, for it is popular demand for salacious information that causes it to be printed, and it is the uncompromising attitude of so many ordinary people towards any individual or family involved in a sex 'scandal' that makes for unnecessary suffering and for a good many suicides.

Deviant sexual behaviour raises the issue of choice and personal responsibility. Relatively few of the girl victims in our study described the offenders in terms suggestive of exclusive paedophilia, that is a fixed preference for the sexually immature, which leaves the individual no choice but children, if he is to have any sexual outlet. Many of the known offenders were relatives or neighbours with children of their own, which implies that they were capable of relations with adults and might, without great sacrifice to themselves, have avoided contact with children. Few of the women in the study thought the behaviour 'unnatural', more of them used the stock phrase 'men are like that', seeming to think that the offenders were yielding to understandable masculine temptations which should have been resisted.

In view of the fact that many of the reported experiences occurred when the respondents were definitely prepubertal, it is open to doubt that all of the offenders were 'normal', in the sense of having nothing more than the average adult male's range of sexual interests. If some of them were compulsive paedophiles, or if they had unusually pronounced paedophile propensities, then the suggestion by a few of the women that some form of 'treatment' might be indicated may not have been altogether inappropriate. The comments on one or two domestic offenders, to the effect that they were known to have offended against children elsewhere, points to the possibility of an overlap between intrafamilial or incestuous child molestation and molestation by strangers. The two phenomena are often assumed to be distinct, but may not always be so.

The homosexual respondents' descriptions of the development of their sexual preference suggested that in many cases an exclusive interest in their own sex had become obvious, and sometimes appeared to be well established, in their early teens or even sooner, apparently without their having any conscious control over the process. But this was not invariable, and some men described considerable heterosexual interest and experience before concluding that their preference was definitely homosexual. This difference in sexual histories is used by some authorities to distinguish two categories of homosexual, the primary and the secondary, the former being possibly innate, perhaps biologically determined, the latter being socially acquired and possibly more a matter of choice. It is sometimes suggested that association with the gay subculture, with its ideas of exclusiveness and separate identity, serves to reinforce an exclusive sexual preference, but most of our own respondents appeared to have been well aware of the direction of their sexual feelings before exposing themselves to the 'gay scene'. The way the sample was selected may have favoured the inclusion of primary more than secondary types. Be that as it may, whatever others might think, few of the respondents appeared to accept personal choice or moral responsibility for their own sexual preference.

Choice seemed likely to be more relevant to the behaviour of the homosexual 'offenders'. None of the homosexual respondents was immune from social pressures, the prospect of discrimination or attempts at moral or financial blackmail, but only those who engaged in illegal behaviour (most often sexual acts or importuning in public) were liable to arrest. In so far as many homosexual men found no need and no inclination to obtain sexual satisfaction by such means, and some were rather condemnatory of those who did, it might be thought that the offender group could rather easily have changed their habits if they had so chosen. That may not have been so easy as it seemed, however, for it was noteworthy that men who had been warned or arrested before for using public lavatories for sexual contacts, continued to risk further confrontations. Possibly at times of loneliness, or in the absence of a regular sexual partner, the lure of readily available sexual contacts, at no cost in money or commitment, seemed to be irresistable to men who had early in their lives learned to find easy release in this way. The outsider may rather too readily mistake a learned dependency for a wilful flouting of authority.

Sexual involvement of children with adults was a topic that came up in the homosexual enquiry as well as in the female victim study. When the homosexual men looked back upon their own childhood, some of them remembered having had contacts with older males, but invariably these contacts were recalled as having either been deliberately sought out or welcomed and responded to with pleasure. This stark contrast with the descriptions of the interviewed women calls for an explanation. Maybe these boys, being already so inclined, found contacts with older males experienced in homosexual activities more interesting and rewarding (and possibly safer from disclosure) than contacts with male peers. If so, their reactions were different from those of most of the respondents in the women's study, who by analogy might have been expected to welcome the attentions of older heterosexual males, but who in fact looked back on such experiences with distaste and anger. Perhaps the two sexes do have fundamentally different reactions to sexual encounters at an early age. Another possible explanation is an opposite bias in the two sets of respondents. Homosexuals wanting to counter the belief that they are potential corrupters of youth might wish to emphasise the willingness of the boy. Women talking to a female interviewer might be inclined to underplay the girl's role. This seems unlikely to be a complete explanation, however, in view of the amount of detail in and apparent frankness of the descriptions given by both sets of informants.

There is a great lack of information about the incidence of sexual contacts between ordinary boys and adults of either sex. Finkelhor's American surveys, which included males, suggested that the majority of boys (necessarily mostly heterosexual) were less upset by approaches from older females than by the attentions of older males. What is needed is a comparison of the recollections of childhood of homosexual and heterosexual adults of both sexes. This might go some way to elucidating the role, if any, of seduction by adults in the determination of sexual orientation. Such an investigation might confirm or refute the curious yet popular assumptions that homosexual approaches to boys or girls are dangerously stimulating and liable to promote sexual deviation, whereas young girls find the heterosexual attentions of their elders unpleasant and liable to cause permanent aversion to men, whilst heterosexual approaches to young boys have no particular significance. As was remarked at the beginning, and is the favourite cry of researchers, our results point the need for further research. In this case the cry seems justified.

Bibliography

SEXUAL MOLESTATION OF YOUNG GIRLS: A RETROSPECTIVE SURVEY

Ariés, P., (1962), Centuries of Childhood, Jonathan Cape,
   London.
Baker, T., (1983), '19' - Incest Survey, unpublished report.
BASPCAN, (1981), Child Sexual Abuse, The British Association
   for the Study and Prevention of Child Abuse and Neglect,
   Rochdale.
Bender, L. and Blau, A., (1937), 'The reaction of children to
   sexual relations with adults', American Journal of
   Orthopsychiatry, vol.7, pp.500-18.
Brongersma, E., (1977), 'On loving relationships human and
   humane', Children's Rights, vol.1.
Brongersma, E., (1980), 'The meaning of "indecency" with
   respect to moral offences involving children', British
   Journal of Criminology, vol.20, no.1, pp.20-34.
Browning, D.H. and Boatman, B., (1977), 'Incest: children at
   risk', American Journal of Psychiatry, vol.134, no.1,
   pp.69-72.
Buchanan, F., (1983), personal communication - letter.
Burton, L., (1968), Vulnerable Children, Routledge and Kegan
   Paul, London.
Card, R., (1975), 'Sexual relations with minors', Criminal Law
   Review, July, pp.370-80.
Chaneles, S., (1967), 'Child victims of sexual offences',
   Federal Probation, vol.31, pp.52-6.

Constantine, L.L., (1981), 'The Effects of Early Sexual Experience: a review and synthesis of research', in Constantine, L.L. and Martinson, F.M., (eds.), (1981), Children and Sex, Little, Brown and Co., Boston (Mass.).

Corwen, D., (1982), talk given at BASPCAN conference, 7.4.82.

De Francis, V., (ed.), (1967), Sexual Abuse of Children, Children's Division of the American Humane Association, Denver.

De Francis, V., (1969), Protecting the Child Victim of Sex Crimes Committed by Adults, Children's Division of the American Humane Association, Denver.

De Mause, (1974), The History of Childhood, Psychohistory Press, New York.

De Young, M., (1982), The Sexual Victimization of Children, McFarland, London.

Finkelhor, D., (1979), Sexually Victimized Children, Free Press, New York.

Finkelhor, D., (1982a), Child Sexual Abuse in a Sample of Boston Families, Family Violence Research Program, New Hampshire.

Finkelhor, D., (1982b), Public Knowledge and Attitudes about Child Sexual Abuse: a Boston survey, Family Violence Research Program, New Hampshire.

Ford, C.S. and Beach, F.A., (1952), Patterns of Sexual Behaviour, Eyre and Spottiswoode, London.

Forward, S. and Buck, C., (1981), Betrayal of Innocence: Incest and its Devastation, Penguin, Harmondsworth.

Fraser, B.G., (1981), 'Sexual Child Abuse: legislation and law in the US', in Mrazek, P.B. and Kempe, C.H., (eds.), (1981), Sexually Abused Children and their Families, Pergamon Press, Oxford.

Gagnon, J.H., (1965), 'Female child victims of sex offences', Social Problems, vol.13, pp.176-92.

Gibbens, J.C.N. and Prince, J., (1963), Child Victims of Sex Offences, Institute for the Study and Treatment of Delinquency, London.

Gittleson, N.L., Eacott, S.E. and Mehta, B.M., (1978), 'Victims of indecent exposure', British Journal of Psychiatry, vol.132, pp.61-6.

Goodwin, J., (ed.), (1982), Sexual Abuse: incest victims and their families, John Wright, Boston (Mass.).

Goodwin, J., McCarty, T. and Divasto, P. (1982), 'Physical and Sexual Abuse of the Children of Adult Incest Victims', in Goodwin, J., (ed.), (1982), Sexual Abuse: incest victims and their families, John Wright, Boston (Mass.).

Goodwin, J. and Owen, J., (1982), 'Incest from Infancy to Adulthood: a developmental approach to victims and families', in Goodwin, J., (ed.), (1982), Sexual Abuse: incest victims and their families, John Wright, Boston

(Mass.).

Greenland, C., (1958), 'Incest', British Journal of
Delinquency, vol.9, pp.62-5.

Hamilton, G.V., (1929), A Research in Marriage, Albert and
Charles Boni, New York.

Herman, J.L., (1981), Father-Daughter Incest, Harvard
University Press, Cambridge (Mass.).

Home Office, (1983), Criminal Statistics England and Wales
1982, HMSO, London.

James, J. and Meyerding, J., (1978), 'Early sexual enterprise
as a factor in prostitution', Archives of Sexual Behaviour,
vol.7, pp.31-42.

Janus, S.S. and Bess, B.E., (1981), 'Latency: fact or
fiction?', in Constantine, L.L. and Martinson, F.M., (eds.),
(1981), Children and Sex, Little, Brown and Co., Boston
(Mass.).

Justice, B. and Justice, R., (1979), The Broken Taboo: Sex in
the Family, Human Sciences Press, New York.

Kapardis, A., (1982), Indecent Exposure: a survey of victims
in Melbourne, unpublished paper.

Kempe, R.S. and Kempe, C.H., (1978), Child Abuse, Fontana,
London.

Kinsey, A.C., Pomeroy, W.B. and Martin, C.E., (1949), Sexual
Behaviour in the Human Male, W.B. Saunders and Co.,
Philadelphia.

Kinsey, A.C., Pomeroy, W.B., Martin, C.E. and Gebhard, P.H.,
(1953), Sexual Behaviour in the Human Female, W.B. Saunders
and Co., Philadelphia.

Kutchinsky, B., (1970), Studies on Pornography and Sex Crimes
in Denmark, New Social Science Monographs, Copenhagen.

Lafon, R., Trivas, J., Faure, J.L. and Pouget, R., (1961),
'Victimologie et criminologie des attentats sexuels sur les
enfants et les adolescents', Annales de Médecine Légale de
Criminologie et de Police Scientifique, vol.41.

Landis, J.T., (1956), 'Experiences of 500 children with adult
sexual deviants', Psychiatric Quarterly Supplement, vol.30,
no.1, pp.91-109.

Lukianowicz, N., (1972), 'Incest', British Journal of
Psychiatry, vol.120, pp.301-13.

Maisch, H., (1973), Incest, Deutsch, London.

Meiselman, K.C., (1978), Incest, Jossey Bass, San Francisco.

Modarressi, T., (1980), 'Personality Development and
Sexuality', in Wolman, B.B. and Money, J., (eds.), (1980),
Handbook of Human Sexuality, Prentice-Hall, Englewood Cliffs.

Mohr, J.W., Turner, R.E. and Jerry, M.B., (1964), Paedophilia
and Exhibitionism, Toronto University Press, Toronto.

Mohr, J.W., (1981), 'Age Structures in Paedophilia', in Cook,
M. and Howells, K., (eds.) (1981), Adult Sexual Interest in
Children, Academic Press, London.

Mrazek, P.B., Lynch, M. and Bentovim, A., (1981), 'Recognition
of Child Sexual Abuse in the United Kingdom', in Mrazek, P.B.
and Kempe, C.H., (eds.), (1981), Sexually Abused Children
and their Families, Pergamon Press, Oxford.

Mrazek, P.B. and Mrazek, D.A., (1981), 'The Effects of Child
Sexual Abuse', in Mrazek, P.B. and Kempe, C.H., (eds.),
(1981), Sexually Abused Children and their Families,
Pergamon Press, Oxford.

Nelson, S., (1982), Incest: fact and myth, Stramullion,
Edinburgh.

Newman, L., (1982), 'The terrors of sexual abuse...behind
closed doors', '19', September, pp.34-6.

Newman, L., (1983), 'Sexual abuse within the family', '19',
May, pp.35-9.

Nie, N.H. et al., (1981), Statistical Package for the Social
Sciences, McGraw-Hill, New York.

O'Carroll, T., (1980), Paedophilia: the radical case, Peter
Owen, London.

Oremland, E. and Oremland, J., (1977), The Sexual and Gender
Development of Young Children: the role of education,
Ballinger, Cambridge (Mass.).

Peters, J.J., (1976), 'Children who are victims of sexual
assault and the psychology of offenders', American Journal
of Psychotherapy, vol.30, pp.398-421.

Powell, G.E. and Chalkley, A.J., (1981), 'The Effects of
Paedophile Attention on the Child', in Taylor, B. (ed.),
(1981), Perspectives on Paedophilia, Batsford, London.

Reifen, D., (1957), 'Sexual offences against children - a new
method of investigation in Israel', World Mental Health,
vol.9, May, pp.74-82.

Reifen, D., (1958), 'The child as a victim of sexual offence:
a new method of investigation in Israel', British Journal of
Psychiatric Social Work, vol.4, no.3.

Reifen, D., (1973), 'Court Procedures in Israel to Protect
Child-Victims of Sexual Assaults', in Drapkin, I. and Viano,
E., (eds.), (1973), Victimology: a new focus, vol.3,
D.C. Heath, Lexington (Mass.).

Renvoize, J., (1982), Incest: a family pattern, Routledge and
Kegan Paul, London.

Rosenfeld, A.A. et al., (1977), 'Incest and sexual abuse of
children', Journal of Child Psychiatry, vol.16, pp.327-39.

Russell, D.E.N., (1983), 'The incidence and prevalence of
intrafamilial sexual abuse of female children', Child Abuse
and Neglect, vol.7, pp.133-46.

Schofield, M., (1965), The Sexual Behaviour of Young People,
Longmans, London.

Scottish Women's Aid Incest Group, (1983), Information Pack on
Incest, Scottish Women's Aid, Dundee.

Silbert, M.H. and Pines, A.M., (1981), 'Sexual child abuse as
an antecedent to prostitution', Child Abuse and Neglect,

vol.5, pp.407-11.

Steele, B.F. and Alexander, H., (1981), 'Long-Term Effects of Sexual Abuse in Childhood', in Mrazek, P.B. and Kempe, C.H., (eds.), (1981), Sexually Abused Children and their Families, Pergamon Press, Oxford.

Taylor, B., (ed.), (1981), Perspectives on Paedophilia, Batsford, London.

Tormes, Y., (1968), Child Victims of Incest, Children's Division of the American Humane Association, Denver.

Virkkunen, M., (1975), 'Victim-precipitated paedophilia offences', British Journal of Criminology, vol.15, no.2, pp.175-80.

Virkkunen, M., (1981), 'The child as participating victim', in Cook, M. and Howells, K., (eds.), (1981), Adult Sexual Interest in Children, Academic Press, London.

Walmsley, R. and White, K., (1979), Sexual Offences, Consent and Sentencing, HMSO, London.

Weinberg, S.K., (1955), Incest Behaviour, Citadel, New York.

Weiss, J. et al., (1955), 'A study of girl sex victims', Psychiatric Quarterly, vol.29, pp.1-27.

West, D.J., (1982), Delinquency: Its Roots, Careers and Prospects, Heinemann, London.

Wilson, G. and Cox, D., (1983), The Child Lovers, Peter Owen, London.

SOCIO-LEGAL PROBLEMS OF MALE HOMOSEXUALS IN BRITAIN

Crane, P., (1982), Gays and the Law, Pluto Press, London.

Galloway, B., (ed.), (1983), Prejudice and Pride: Discrimination against Gay People in Modern Britain, Routledge and Kegan Paul, London.

Harris, M., (1973), The Dilly Boys, Croom Helm, London.

Home Office, (1956), Report of the Committee on Homosexual Offences and Prostitution, Cmnd. 247, HMSO, London.

Home Office, (1983), Criminal Statistics England and Wales 1982, HMSO, London.

Humphreys, L., (1970), Tearoom Trade, Duckworth, London.

Meldrum, J., (1979), Attacks on Gay People, Campaign for Homosexual Equality, London.

Meldrum, J. and West, D.J., (1983), 'Homosexual offences as reported in the press', Medicine, Science and the Law, vol.23, pp.41-53.

Miller, B. and Humphreys, L., (1980), 'Lifestyles and violence: homosexual victims of assault and murder', Journal of Qualitative Sociology, vol.3, pp.169-85.

Office of Population Censuses and Surveys, (1982), Labour Force Survey, 1981, (Table 4.27), HMSO, London.

Office of Population Censuses and Surveys, (1984), Labour

Force Survey, HMSO, London.
Westwood, G., (1960), A Minority, Longmans, London.

Appendix

LETTER SENT OUT BY THE COOPERATING G.P.

PLEASE READ THIS LETTER CAREFULLY

Recently newspapers and T.V. programmes have shown that many women have sexual experiences with adults when they are children. Doctors, law-makers and social services want to protect and care appropriately for children who have such experiences today. To do so they need to know how many women this has happened to and how they are affected when they grow up.

I am writing to you to ask for your help in a study which is trying to find the answers to these questions. It is being carried out by Caroline Nash and is funded by the Department of Health. Caroline has talked about the research plans with me and she has my full support for this important work. She is a gentle, sympathetic person who is experienced in talking to women about sexual matters. As she will not have time to talk to all the women on my list, we have taken names at random and yours has come up.

PLEASE HELP US. You can by:

1. Filling in the enclosed questionnaire and returning it anonymously in the envelope provided.

2.   Talking to Caroline (if you are willing please mark your questionnaire accordingly).

If you do not want to help. please return the questionnaire blank with your reasons. We shall not trouble you again.

Anything you tell Caroline will be treated as strictly confidential. Your name will not appear anywhere on the answer sheet and she will not discuss your answers with me. What you say will only be used for research purposes.

WHETHER OR NOT YOU HAD ANY SEXUAL EXPERIENCES AS A CHILD, YOUR VIEWS ARE IMPORTANT. We hope to hear from you soon.

Yours sincerely,

SPECIMEN OF QUESTIONNAIRE

Remember that your answers to these questions will be kept strictly confidential. Please be as honest as you can.

1.   Are you

married ___

single ✓

separated or divorced ___

widowed ___

---

2.   If you ever married please give your age when you first married

_____

---

3.   Please tick all those who live in the same home with you now:

nobody else, I live alone ✓   husband ___

father ___   boyfriend ___

mother ___   child(ren) ___

other (please state) ....

176

4. What is your present occupation?

_____

5. What is the occupation of the main wage-earner in your
    home?

_____

The rest of the questions are about your childhood, that is,
when you were less than 16 years old.

6. What was your father's main occupation when you were a
    child?

_____

7. As a child did you live

                              in the country ____

                              in a small town ____

                    in a large town or city ____

_____

8. How many <u>older</u> brothers and sisters did you have?

                                        Number

                        brothers   ____

                        sisters   ____

_____

9. How many <u>younger</u> brothers and sisters did you have?

                                        Number

                        brothers   ____

                        sisters   ____

_____

10. On the whole do you remember your childhood as being

                        very happy   ____

                        quite happy   ____

                        not very happy ____

177

11. Tick the main sources of your knowledge about sex as a child

mother ___	father ___
brother ___	sister ___
girlfriend ___	boyfriend ___
classes at school ___	other adult relative ___
book or magazine ___	self-discovery ___
T.V. or films ___	don't remember ___
dirty jokes ___	none ___

12. The following statements were made by some women about things which happened to them when they were children. Please tick if any of them happened to you as a child (under 16 years old).
    (Adult means someone at least 5 years older than your-self.)

	Once	More than once
a. I was asked to do something sexual by an adult	___	___
b. I received an obscene phone call	___	___
c. I was kissed by an adult in a sexual way	___	___
d. I saw a 'flasher'	___	___
e. An adult fondled my private parts ..	___	___
f. An adult made me touch their private parts	___	___
g. An adult attempted to have sex with me	___	___
h. An adult had full sexual intercourse		

178

with me .. .. ___   ___

i. If something similar happened, not given
   above, please describe here: ....

   IF NONE OF THESE HAPPENED TO YOU PLEASE TICK HERE ___
   and turn to page 5.

---

13. Was the adult involved

    a stranger ___   a family friend ___

    father ___   other, please state ....

---

14. How old were you when the incident happened? (Give the
    youngest age if you ticked more than one.)

                                              _____

---

15. How do you feel about what happened at the time?

---

16. Did you tell anyone about the incident(s)?

              Yes ___   No ___

    If YES who did you tell?

    What was their reaction?

    Did you find them helpful?

              Yes ___   No ___

---

17. How long did the experience(s) affect you?

                    not at all ___

                  a few weeks ___

               several months ___

               a year or more ___

                still affected ___

179

18. How do you feel about this now?

_____

Thank you for filling in this questionnaire. <u>Whatever you
have answered</u>, it would help our research if you are willing
to talk to Caroline. The choice is yours, but we would like
to explain that by putting together your experiences and opinions with those of others, we can obtain information which can
be used to help other women and children. What you say will
be strictly confidential and we can talk in your home or elsewhere - wherever you feel most comfortable.

If you <u>are</u> willing to talk to Caroline please complete the
following:

My first name is ....
Either 1. Please contact me on telephone no. ....
            to arrange a convenient time and place.
Or   2. I do not have a telephone. Please contact me at
            address: ....
            A convenient day and time would be ....

            If you would like to talk about the research some
            more before deciding, please ring

_____

If you have <u>not</u> completed the questionnaire. Please give your
reasons here:

NOW PLEASE RETURN THE QUESTIONNAIRE IN THE ENVELOPE PROVIDED